365 WAYS TO BE MORE STOIC

365 WAYS TO BE MORE STOIC

TIM LEBON

EDITED BY KASEY PIERCE

First published by John Murray Learning in 2022
An imprint of John Murray Press
A division of Hodder & Stoughton Ltd,
An Hachette UK company

1

Edited by Kasey Pierce

A CIP catalogue record for this title is available from the British Library

Hardback ISBN 978 1 52939 044 5
eBook ISBN 9781529390469

Typeset by KnowledgeWorks Global Ltd.

Printed and bound in Great Britain by Clays Ltd, Elcograf S.p.A.

John Murray Press policy is to use papers that are natural, renewable and recyclable products and made from wood grown in sustainable forests. The logging and manufacturing processes are expected to conform to the environmental regulations of the country of origin.

John Murray Press
Carmelite House
50 Victoria Embankment
London EC4Y 0DZ

www.johnmurraypress.co.uk

To the memory of my parents,

Gee and Sidney

CONTENTS

About the author   ix

Preface   xi

Introduction   xiii

1   What is within your control?   1

2   Happiness and the virtues   21

3   Stoic serenity   43

4   Finding the right direction   63

5   Self-control   83

6   Courage   105

7   Justice   125

8   Wisdom   149

9   Coping with adversity   171

10 On anger management   193

11 The shortness of life   215

12 The next level   237

Epilogue: The 'big five' takeaways   259

References   263

Acknowledgements   267

ABOUT THE AUTHOR

Author

Tim LeBon is an accredited CBT psychotherapist, working in the NHS and in private practice. He is a founding member of Modern Stoicism and is its director of research, and is responsible for running international Stoic Week. Tim's previous books include *Wise Therapy* and *Achieve Your Potential with Positive Psychology*.

Website: www.timlebon.com

YouTube Channel: StoicLifeCoaching

Editor

Kasey Pierce is a freelance writer/editor. An author and editor of comics, Kasey is a follower of Stoicism, a Stoic columnist on *Medium*, has been interviewed on the subject for the Modern Stoicism podcast, and has spoken at the Stoicon-X Women conference on Stoicism and creativity. Kasey is passionate about Stoicism and broadening its appeal to reach a wider audience through her experience as a writer and editor in other genres.

PREFACE

My Stoic journey began in 2012 when I was invited to a workshop on Stoicism. Back then, I wasn't nearly so much into Stoicism, wrongly identifying it with 'sucking it up'.

There I met Chris Gill, John Sellars, Donald Robertson and others who became part of what has become Modern Stoicism. We decided to run an online Stoic Week, where people could 'live like a Stoic' for a week based on readings we supplied. Importantly, we measured participants' well-being – before and after – to learn whether Stoicism actually worked.

We were stunned. Our little experiment attracted more people than we'd anticipated. Many reported significant benefits. Since then, thousands have participated in annual international Stoic Weeks. The initial positive findings have been replicated, consistently.

The more I learned about Stoicism, the more I realized its massive potential. I started to adopt it as my own life philosophy and introduced some Stoic ideas to my clients, who responded very positively.

When asked to write this book, I saw this as a chance to share these ideas with a wider audience. It was important to include real-life stories of how modern Stoicism helps, and I'm so happy to be able to include over 30 such guest contributors. I would like to thank every guest story contributor for their generosity in sharing their Stoic experiences.

I was extremely fortunate that Kasey Pierce was suggested as editor for this book. I thought I was quite good at communicating complex ideas. Kasey takes this to the next level! I would write an entry, send it to Kasey asking her to work her magic on it – and back it would come, so much more relatable. If you find yourself laughing out loud, thank Kasey!

I'd like to thank my wife, Beata, and children, Mike and Katie, for their love and support as well as offering an apology if I seemed a little busy over the last year. I promise to make it up to you!

I would like to thank all my friends and colleagues at Modern Stoicism, the Aurelius Foundation and TalkPlus for their amazing work and support over the years. Chris Gill, who introduced me to Modern Stoicism, has been a consistent fount of wisdom.

I am especially grateful for those, including David Arnaud, Eve Riches, Shamil Chandaria and Peter Cooper, who were kind enough to offer feedback on specific entries or chapters. I take sole responsibility for the views I express.

This book contains a mixture of real-life stories and fictionalized or semi-fictionalized vignettes. Here's how to tell which is which. Where an entry is credited with the author's full name – for instance **82: Stoic forgiveness – John Harlow'**, this is a real story. Where only a first name is given without a credit (e.g. **55: Freya's frustrations**), this is a vignette. Two exceptions are the stories of 'Roy', a client who kindly gave permission to share his story, and 'Shane', a modern Stoic who requested his story be anonymized. Where I've drawn on client work, I've disguised identifying details.

Over 100 Stoic quotations have been selected to illuminate many entries. They've been adapted so they are gender-neutral and, occasionally, for readability.

This book contains 365 lessons on how to be more Stoic. Whether you read one entry a day or binge-read them, I hope that Stoicism helps you as much as it has helped me and my clients.

Tim LeBon

Guildford, May 2022

INTRODUCTION

Happiness, serenity and fulfilment are within your control, and within your power to have. So, too, are constructive ways to handle frustration, adversity and even your own mortality.

This is a guide to help you navigate through the controllable and inevitable, and, ultimately, to a meaningful life, filled with happiness.

This is *365 Ways to Be More Stoic*.

Stoicism is now experiencing a massive resurgence, having struck a chord with seekers of wisdom who value personal improvement based on a solid foundation. This is despite misconceptions about this school of philosophical thought – one of the most popular being that Stoicism is all about 'keeping a stiff upper lip'. That is 'stoicism' with a lowercase 's' and has *nothing whatsoever* to do with the philosophy you will be learning about in these pages. Real Stoics don't button up negative emotions because they don't need to. Stoicism shines a different, more positive light on situations so you don't get so worked up in the first place.

Key Stoic ideas that help us achieve this emotional stability include:

■ Much human misery is self-imposed and depends upon your outlook.

■ Only focus on what you can control, such as your thinking and behaviour.

■ If you develop a good character, leading a happy and fulfilling life becomes easier.

Studies confirm that Stoicism reduces anger and anxiety. Significantly, it also increases enjoyment, optimism, resilience and zest.

Stoicism began in the third century BCE, when Zeno of Citium, a prosperous merchant from Cyprus, was shipwrecked near Athens. Soon after, he happened upon a book of Socratic dialogues that inspired him to devote his life to the pursuit of wisdom, otherwise known as philosophy, rather than material wealth. He lectured publicly in the Stoa Poikile, or Painted Porch, in the Athenian agora. His followers therefore became known as Stoics.

Stoicism was embraced by Romans a century later, becoming popular among the ruling class and even some slaves. Stoics believe that wisdom and happiness are accessible to all.

The 'big three' Stoics, whose ideas you'll be learning about, are Seneca, Epictetus and Marcus Aurelius:

- **Seneca**, born 4 BCE, was an advisor and former tutor to Emperor Nero. Seneca wrote letters full of practical Stoic wisdom to his friends. He also wrote insightful essays to help with anger and time management.
- **Epictetus**, born 55 CE, was a crippled former slave. He wrote nothing, but his lectures were transcribed as *The Discourses* by a student named Arrian, who also distilled key quotes into the briefer *Enchiridion*, or *Handbook of Epictetus*.
- **Marcus Aurelius**, born 121 CE, was both a Roman emperor and a committed Stoic. His personal journal has survived as the *Meditations*.

In the twentieth century, therapists drew on Stoicism to create modern cognitive behavioural therapy (CBT), while self-help groups like Alcoholics Anonymous popularized Stoic-like ideas through the Serenity Prayer.

Recently, top Stoic writers like Massimo Pigliucci, John Sellars and Donald Robertson – whose personal accounts are featured in this book – have further popularized Stoic ideas.

Modern Stoicism, a group of academics and therapists, started the first International Stoic Week in 2012 – in which thousands of people 'live like a Stoic' for a week.

I often wondered: *What if we all lived like a Stoic for more than a week?*

365 Ways to Be More Stoic is my attempt to produce a book that offers guidance in living a wiser, happier and, yes, more Stoic life.

CHAPTER 1

WHAT IS WITHIN YOUR CONTROL?

One of the most powerful Stoic lessons is contained at the very start of the *Enchiridion*, or *Handbook of Epictetus*: 'Some things are within our direct control and other things are not.' We should focus all our energies on those things under our direct control.

So, what, according to the Stoics, is under our direct control? Less than most of us think. Essentially, only what we do and how we think about things. *The problem is we spend so much time trying to control other things*. This inevitably leads to all kinds of serious problems including disappointment, frustration and bad relationships.

In my work as a psychotherapist and life coach, this apparently obvious truth has probably had the most profound impact of all the Stoic ideas. Many clients have found that this key Stoic idea helps with anger management, worry, sleep issues, social anxiety, and dealing with various adversities such as illness and injury, to name a few.

We will be returning to this theme in future chapters, for example those on Stoic serenity, anger and adversity. I hope the introduction to the dichotomy of control in this chapter lays a solid foundation to you becoming more Stoic and at the same time a calmer, more rational version of yourself.

1   Control the controllables

After winning her match in the 2021 US Open quarter-finals, 18-year-old outsider Emma Raducanu was asked the secret of how she, such a young and inexperienced player, could look so composed on the court.

'Control the controllables, be in the moment and concentrate on the next point' came the reply.

Three days later, Raducanu made history by becoming the first qualifier *ever* to win a grand slam.

'Controlling the controllables' has become a byword for top sportspeople. It also happens to be the simplest way to express the fundamental truth put forward by Epictetus at the start of the *Handbook*. Its application is by no means confined to elite sport.

When you concentrate on the things you can control – such as being in the present moment and what you do next – you become more focused, calm and effective.

When you focus on things outside of your control, your attention is scattered, you become more anxious and less effective.

Think back over the last 24 hours. How could controlling the controllables have helped you?

2   Coach A and Coach B

Imagine two tennis coaches.

Coach A offers this advice:

Try to stop the crowd from cheering for your opponent. Reflect on how rotten your luck has been. Pray that your opponent gets tired.

Coach B offers very different advice:

Focus all your energy on your next shot and how best you can play it. Ignore the crowd. Forget everything that has gone before and focus on the present moment.

We know that coach B is offering much sounder advice, but why? Reflect on the why and ready yourself for its practical application when you find yourself in a pressing moment – at work or in the home – today.

3 What you can and can't control: a self-check-in

Trying to control what you can't may become a non-stop cycle of frustration and disappointment. If, instead, you focus on what you can control, you will feel more positive and be much more efficient.

Get ahead of the day, and this cycle, and perform this brief self-check-in:

- What is on your mind today?
- What aspects of these things can you control?
- What can't you control?

4 The Stoic solution: the dichotomy of control

Some things are within your control and others are not.

Under your control are what you do and the way you think about things.

Everything else – what others do, what they think about you, the past and the outcome of your actions – is not under your control.

This 'dichotomy of control' gives a Stoic spin to controlling the controllables.

Focus only on your actions and thoughts.

Don't let anything not under your control upset you.

That's the way to Stoic serenity.

5 The dichotomy of control comes to my rescue

I found a great opportunity to practise the dichotomy of control when I lost my wallet shortly before I was due to travel abroad. My first reaction was to be furious with myself for letting it happen. Then I remembered Stoicism.

What couldn't I control? *That the wallet had gone.*

What could I control? *I could ring the bank.*

What could I learn from it? *To be more careful in future.*

My new credit cards arrived in time for my travel, and Stoicism helped me deal with the situation calmly and rationally. When we take a logical point of view, we become less panicky. That clarity allows us to see that the solution to this problem is simply, well, simple!

6 Heather has a blind date!

Heather has a blind date tonight and she's nervous. Can Stoicism help her out?

Which of these are within her control and which are not?

a. Whether her date will be her 'type'

b. Whether *she* will be their 'type'

c. If the date goes well, whether they'll be happy together

d. Having a positive attitude towards her date

The answer? Only d.

Once Heather lets go and stops worrying about the things she cannot control, she feels calmer and begins to actually feel excited about the evening.

7 Another weekend

It's Saturday morning and Paula is starting to feel blue. Nothing is going her way. Her boss doesn't appreciate her, she is sure she flunked a recent job interview, and her lover hasn't responded to her suggestions for date night.

Then she remembers Stoicism and controlling the controllables.

She uses this simple three-column technique to get over the weekend blues, remembering that all she can control are her thoughts and actions.

Issue	Can't control	Action plan
Work	Boss	?
Interview	What happened	?
Love life	Lover	?

What do you think would be a Stoic approach for her going forward? Help Paula by entering a wise plan of action into the last column.

8 Saturday serenity

Here's how Paula used Stoicism to help turn her weekend around.

Issue	Can't control	Action plan
Work	Boss	Accept not being appreciated, become indifferent to it, and look for a new satisfying position.
Interview	What happened	I don't know for sure that I didn't get the job. If I didn't, I'll reflect on what I can learn from the interview experience.
Love life	Lover	Well, if he's not interested in me, then I can't change that. It is what it is and his perception of me does not determine my value.

Do you agree with her action plans?

Try out the same three-column technique today to achieve Stoic serenity, every day.

9   The Serenity Prayer

In recovery programmes, the first lines of the Serenity Prayer are traditionally recited at the start of every meeting:

> God, grant me the serenity to accept the things
> I cannot change, courage to change the things I can,
> and wisdom to know the difference.

Fun fact – the seeds of the Serenity Prayer can be seen in Epictetus's *Handbook* written nearly two thousand years ago! Regardless of your beliefs, 'God' can be viewed as what directs you – whatever power motivates and drives you personally. It's a very memorable way of expressing the dichotomy of control.

Use this mantra as a serene reminder to wisely discern what you can and cannot control, so as to avoid disturbing your inner peace.

10   'But I want to have an impact on the world'

Harry very much likes the idea that he will feel tranquil once he lets go of everything outside his control. But he is concerned that Stoicism might mean he accepts too much and becomes passive, and so not an agent for change.

'I don't want to accept the world stoically! I want to help make the world a better place!' he cries.

This is a misconception, confusing lowercase stoicism (keeping a 'stiff upper lip') with uppercase Stoicism – *real* Stoicism! Ancient Stoics like the Roman senator Cato the Younger were *very* involved in politics. Stoicism isn't about being passive at all. In fact, it's all about doing the right thing when it's time for action and embracing radical acceptance when it's not.

The Serenity Prayer captures this part of Stoicism memorably.

Real Stoics have the courage to change what they can (and should) change and the serenity to accept what they truly cannot.

11   What about things you can *influence*?

Ricky, a Stoic novice, isn't so sure that the Stoics have got it right:

'Shouldn't there be a third category – things that you haven't got full control over but can still influence? For example, I want to request time off work. I agree it's not completely under my control, but surely I have *some* influence over the outcome, right?'

'And how would you best influence the outcome?' replies Sam, Ricky's friend and a more experienced Stoic.

'By the way I make my case,' answers Ricky.

'Can you control how you make your case?' asks Sam.

'For sure.'

'Can you control whether your boss approves your request?'

'Not really.'

'Then influence the outcome by focusing fully on what you can control – your actions.'

It all comes back to the dichotomy of control. Sure, we can influence things, but we best do this by focusing only on those aspects that are under our direct control.

12   The Stoic Archer

The Stoics came up with a super-helpful analogy to help us further understand the dichotomy of control – that of an archer. Archery is an outdoor sport, so we know the archer's performance is vulnerable to the elements. This would include the wind, of course. So even when an archer fires a 'perfect' shot, they still might miss. A gust of wind might blow the arrow off course, an external factor the archer can't control.

Here's the question:

What attitude should the archer take if they do everything right but then the wind makes them miss?

The Stoic answer is to be unconcerned.

As long as you did your best, you should not blame yourself for the outcome if an external, uncontrollable factor blows you off course.

I find that a very reassuring idea, don't you?

13 'Be the Stoic Archer, Dad'

From Scott Corey of Stoic Archer Academy LLC – mental health coach, Stoic mentor, substance use clinician

My son, at eight years old, tried his hand at archery for the first time. He was sincerely enjoying just shooting the arrows at the ground and hoping they would stick. I asked him to shoot for a goal and aim for a target. Just a few misses and my son let out an audible sigh of disappointment. I taught him the Stoic Archer's lesson: the dichotomy of control and its benefits, the dangers of outcome-based thinking, the importance of practising doing your best in everything you do and how *that* is what truly matters. Now, when I strive for goals, my son says to me: 'Be the Stoic Archer, Dad.'

14 A problem with goals

Tom wants to lose weight. His doctor has advised him that he needs to lose a significant amount, but he feels overwhelmed by the prospect.

He flits between avoiding dieting altogether and going on crash diets that he can't sustain.

Sound familiar?

The Stoic approach to setting goals can help Tom and others feel more in control. It has two key steps:

1. Define what needs to be done to achieve your outcome.
2. Make sure the steps are within your control.

What is within Tom's control as he sets out on his weight loss journey?

15 Tom's Stoic diet

The Stoic approach to setting goals is to focus on the *process* more than the outcome. The process, the journey, is under our control; the outcome is not.

Tom lays out his plan of action:

- Meal and snack prepping for the week
- Avoiding processed junk foods
- Setting a reasonable calorie limit
- Moderate exercise
- Talking to a trusted friend about the plan

He is excited by this plan but pauses to ask whether his action plan is made up of things within his control. For a Stoic sage – yes! But his self-knowledge tells him that he would struggle with the avoiding junk food part. So, he moderates this rule – one takeaway a week is allowed so long as he follows all the other rules.

Three months later, Tom is happy to report that his Stoic diet is going very well. What do you think of this approach?

16   Your Stoic step-by-step plan

Is there anything you would like to achieve that feels a bit daunting? Would you like to try a Stoic goal-setting approach? You can apply Tom's approach to nearly any goal!

Make your Stoic step-by-step plan below. It will only take five minutes and you'll be glad you did!

The outcome I want to achieve is …

_____

_____

_____

_____

The steps I need to take each day to achieve this are …

1. _____

2. _____

3. _____

4. _____

The most common trap is to make the steps too ambitious – things that might be in your control if you were a Stoic sage but aren't realistic for you … *yet!*

Tip: Prefer baby steps to big steps. For example, if your goal is to exercise more but you are finding it difficult to find time between school, work or the kids, prefer increasing your step-count each day. Even getting in some laps around the block can be worked into the busiest of schedules.

These baby steps are steps within our control and a precursor to larger achievements. With each success, confidence and ability grow.

17   Use the reserve clause

When stating goals, ancient Stoics would often add phrases like 'fate permitting' or 'unless anything prevents me'.

Why? Because then they weren't setting themselves up for expecting outcomes outside of their control and subsequent disappointment. This is called adding a reserve clause.

So why not experiment yourself? Try:

> 'I will see you tomorrow – *fate permitting*' or

> 'I will go on holiday next month – *unless anything prevents me*.'

Alternative reserve clauses might be 'God willing', 'if all goes well' or 'other things being equal'.

Which reserve clause resonates the most with you?

18   The true cause of unhappiness?

In his excellent book *Lessons in Stoicism*, John Sellars, a leading Modern Stoic scholar, makes the startling claim that much unhappiness is down to us misclassifying things as being under our control when they are not.

It's worth rereading that sentence.

If true, it means Stoicism can make a *huge* positive difference to you.

Could it be true for you?

Do any of the things that cause you unhappiness stem from you thinking that you have control over things you don't?

19 Unhappiness – a psychotherapist's perspective

As a psychotherapist, the more I explored Stoicism, the more I realized this ancient philosophy is incredibly relatable to my modern-day clients. Going back through my caseload, I see many problems lead back to the same root cause: trying to control the uncontrollable.

Anger and frustration – *believing you can control other people*

Shame and guilt – *believing you had more control over the past*

Worry and anxiety – *overthinking aspects of the future you cannot control*

Procrastination – *trying to get everything perfect before you start – you can't make everything perfect*

and this was just a start …

Are the concerns that brought my clients to therapy relevant to you?

Could the dichotomy of control help you manage them better?

20 Worrying about things outside your control

Are you a worrier? If so, the dichotomy of control can come to the rescue.

Simply ask yourself – am I worrying about things outside my control?

If the answer is yes, ignore the worry – it's outside your control, so why fritter away your energy worrying about it?

On the other hand, if you are worrying about things that *are* under your control, then act or make a plan. It's as simple as that.

Consider these three cases. In each case, should you ignore the worry, act or plan?

1. The possibility of a financial crash next year

2. Having an interview tomorrow

3. Anxiety about missing your flight

You'll find each of these worries covered in the remaining entries in this chapter.

Today, when you notice yourself worrying, simply ask yourself what you're worried about. If it's about something you cannot control, don't worry.

21   Choose the right time to worry

> 'Often things that appear terrible during the night,
> seem ridiculous in the morning.'
>
> Seneca, *Letters* 114.24

We cannot control whether a worrying thought comes into our mind. We can, however, choose *when* to deal with it.

There are times, when we're tired or very emotional, when experience tells us worrying about something isn't going to help. We are simply going to go over things repeatedly, leading us nowhere but to anxiety.

What people often try to do is block the worrying thought or push it away. This is counterproductive: like a beach ball pushed under water, the worry tends to come back to the surface, only with more force.

A much better strategy is to *postpone the worry* to a time when you're better able to think rationally about the issue.

Modern CBT therapists often recommend worriers postpone their worries to an agreed *worry time*. This is a period of 15 minutes or so when you are allowed to worry as much as you like. At all other times, worrying is banned, though you are allowed to jot down the worry for later, so you don't forget.

When would be the right time for you to choose to worry?

22   How to ignore a worry

'It's all very well telling me to ignore a worry when it's about something beyond my control, but that doesn't make it go away.'

Brian's concern is a very common one. The trick is *not* to try to make it go away, but to let the worry still be there, and instead to focus your attention on something else. That way it eventually loses its force.

If the worry happens in the daytime, get really immersed in something – such as a game, a conversation with a friend, exercise, whatever works for you.

If it's when you're trying to fall asleep, a helpful idea is to play the 'ABC game'. This involves going through the alphabet, thinking of boys' names, girls' names, countries of the world … it really doesn't matter what: the purpose is just to take your mind off the worry.

23   Stoic mantras to reduce worry

Some people find it helpful to recall and recite to themselves a Stoic saying to prevent them boarding the worry train. Here are some of my favourites:

'We are more often upset by our own minds than by reality.'

Seneca, *Letters* 1.43

'Today I escaped difficulties, or rather I cast them out, for they were not outside me, but within, in my judgements.'

Marcus Aurelius, *Meditations* 9.13

'If it concerns anything not in our control, be prepared to say that it is nothing to you.'

Handbook of Epictetus 1

Which of these could you try today if you noticed yourself engaged in unproductive worry?

24   Worrying makes me a good person ...

Carrie, a mother of two typical teenagers, has come to therapy because her worrying is having an impact on her well-being and relationships, but is reluctant to stop.

'It's natural to worry about my girls when its 11:00 pm and they aren't home. What mother wouldn't?'

The Stoic answer is that while it's natural – and outside our control – to be *concerned*, we don't have to be *worried*.

'So, Carrie ...' I began. 'Suppose you had a sleep problem. Imagine two versions of me as your therapist. Therapist 1 tells you that I had spent the whole week worrying about your sleep problem. Therapist 2 comes with a list of useful ideas to help you sleep. Which therapist would you choose?'

'Obviously therapist 2.'

'So, it's not the worrying that you value, it's my giving your concern some thought and coming up with something that's useful. Does you worrying about your girls actually *help* anyone?'

'No, it just gets me anxious and annoyed with them for making me anxious! As soon as they walk in the door, we start shouting at each other!'

So much for worrying making someone a good person ...

25   A man of action?

Roddy is also unsure about whether to give up worrying and has a different objection:

'Saying a Stoic mantra to himself might have worked for Seneca, but I'm a man of action!'

'Are you sure you are being a man of action when you are worrying?' I reply.

'Umm, I see what you mean, but surely there are some occasions when you really do need to do something?'

'Exactly. It's all about separating out the aspects of a situation that are within your control – that's where you need action – and those that are not under your control, which you need to accept. For example, if you have a plane to catch tomorrow, worrying about it is only likely to mean you won't be well rested. Instead, make a plan to set off early, which is under your control. The action required is in productive thinking, not in worrying.'

26   The Stoic Worry Tree

The Stoic Worry Tree brings together all these ideas about how the dichotomy of control can help you manage worry in one place.

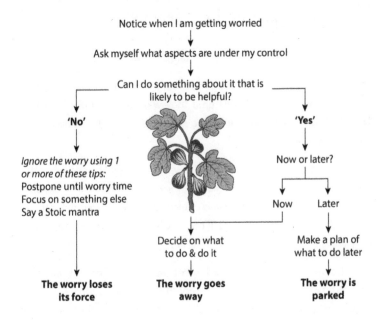

Notice when I am getting worried

Ask myself what aspects are under my control

Can I do something about it that is likely to be helpful?

'No'

Ignore the worry using 1 or more of these tips:
Postpone until worry time
Focus on something else
Say a Stoic mantra

The worry loses its force

Decide on what to do & do it

The worry goes away

'Yes'

Now or later?

Now   Later

Make a plan of what to do later

The worry is parked

For example, Janet is worried about whether she will get laid off work. She decides there is nothing she can do about it, so she follows the left-hand side of the tree. She recites the Stoic mantra, 'We suffer more often in imagination than in reality' and the worry loses its force.

Kate is worried that she will get fined as her parking ticket is about to expire. She decides to end her shopping expedition, returns to the car and the worry goes away.

Gary is worried about an economic downturn. He realizes that he cannot control the situation but he can control his savings. He makes a plan to contact his financial advisor. The worry is parked.

Many of my clients have found the Stoic Worry Tree helpful; some even print it out so they can be reminded of it every day. Do you think it might help you?

27   Stoicism for interview nerves

From Megan Brown – Research Fellow in Medical Education

I had an interview recently for a job I really wanted. I usually suffer from pre-interview nerves, but this time they were almost unbearable. The week before, relaxing was difficult because I always felt I could be doing more to prepare.

A couple of days before the interview, I realized just how exhausted I was. I decided to stop and reflect on how much I had done already to prepare, and on what I could and could not control about the interview. I thought of practical things I could do to ease my mind, such as preparing an outfit the night before and having my CV printed.

This helped, but what helped most was reminding myself of the *dichotomy of control*. I couldn't control what questions I would be asked, how the interviewers would act, or even whether my internet connection would behave. I had done what I could to prepare, and I found peace and reassurance in this thought that served me well during the interview. And I got the job!

28   A good night's sleep

Many of us struggle with sleep problems. The dichotomy of control can often help. We can't control the moment we drop off to sleep. So, obsessive thoughts such as 'It's 2 am and I'm still not asleep' are very unhelpful. However, we can create the conditions that make it more likely we have a good night's sleep. Here is a list of good sleep hygiene tips that you have control over:

- Exercise in the day – but not too close to bedtime.
- Limit caffeine intake, especially in the evening.
- Limit alcohol consumption – alcohol is sedating but damages our nervous system and gives us poor-quality sleep.
- Have a relaxing wind-down routine, such as reading a book, listening to relaxing music or having a bath and avoiding screens of any kind.
- Make sure you have a comfortable, quiet environment for sleep.

Could taking control of the right things help you get a good night's sleep?

29   Don't sweat the small stuff

From Lori Huica – Stoic Survival and Resilience Facilitator for the Aurelius Foundation

A few small (but cumulatively significant) things used to cause me stress: poor internet connection during work video calls, frequent and unexpected delays on the Underground, outside construction noise during calls …

Then I began to ask myself, 'Am I really in control of these external stressors?' Of course, I wasn't. Now I just think, 'Well, OK!', and carry on with my day, putting less emotional investment in uncontrollable passing moments. Small tweaks in your perception add up.

30   What can you control?

Often, we go wrong by overestimating what we can control. But sometimes we forget the simplest things we do have control over – such as ...

■ If a relationship is struggling, talk about it with your partner.

■ If something you've tried hasn't worked, try to understand why.

■ If a friend hasn't called you back, suspend judgement about the reason.

Pick an area you would like to improve and find one thing that you have control over – and do it!

Follow-up

■ Revisit 3: What you can and can't control: a self-check-in. Compare your answers now with those you gave earlier.

■ The essential entry from this chapter is 4: The Stoic solution: the dichotomy of control. Read this again and as often as you can.

■ Try sharing one or more of the practical ideas in this chapter with friends, colleagues or family.

CHAPTER 2
HAPPINESS AND THE VIRTUES

You have two minutes to answer these two key questions:

1. How can I be happy?
2. How can I lead a good and worthwhile life?

Were your answers to these two questions very different?

Many people contrast being happy, which they equate with pleasure, with leading a meaningful life, which they assume means helping others and sacrificing one's own happiness.

The Stoics challenge this way of thinking. They believe that the paths to happiness and to a good life are identical. This is very good news indeed. You can be happy, without guilt or a lack of meaning.

So how, according to the Stoics, can you do this?

In this chapter, you'll discover the answer.

The short answer is that the trick is to learn about and then adopt certain internal qualities, called *virtues*.

According to the Stoics, there are four main virtues, and lots of lesser virtues as well. The chief virtue is wisdom. The dichotomy of control, which you now know all about from Chapter 1, is a key part of wisdom. The other main virtues are justice (which is much broader than just fairness and includes love and compassion), courage and self-control.

In this chapter you will learn about the virtues in general and why they're so important. Later chapters will home in on each of the four main virtues.

31   The best path to happiness

> 'Very little indeed is necessary for living a happy life.'
>
> Marcus Aurelius, *Meditations* 7.67

Everyone wants to be happy. But what is the best path to happiness? Is it pursuing ...

a. Pleasure and fun?

b. Achievement and status?

c. Money and material goods?

d. Rationality and virtue?

If you answered d), then you may well be a natural Stoic! Rationality helps you decide what you need to do to be happy; virtue means you have the right motivation.

Can you see any problems with the (non-Stoic) answers a), b) and c)?

If d) is the best path to happiness, what difference can this make to the choices you make today?

32   The myth of King Midas

'For what else is tragedy but the dramatized sufferings of people, bewildered by an admiration of externals?'

Epictetus, *Discourses* 1.4.26

Granted one wish, King Midas asked that everything he touch be turned into gold.

Unfortunately, this apparent blessing turned out to be a great curse: when Midas tried to eat, the food turned to gold as soon as it touched his tongue. In some versions of the story, he starved to death. In others, Midas hugged his beloved daughter, and she turned into a gold statue.

When I have asked students to name the moral of the story, three answers recur:

- Don't be greedy.
- Don't be materialistic.
- All that glitters is not gold.

The Stoic would agree with all of these, and add one more vital lesson:

■ Don't overvalue external things like wealth, status and pleasure.

Take a moment to write down some *internals* you're grateful for, the things money can't buy, such as your ability to take a step back and think things through, to decide what to value and to choose your attitudes.

33   All that glitters …

'If only I could afford that holiday …'

'If only I got that job …'

'If only I could work up the courage to ask them out …'

Which of these *if onlys* have you indulged in? When you got them, did that holiday, job or lover actually bring you lasting happiness?

Today's challenge is to make a list of all the things in your life that glittered and turned out not to be so golden.

Perhaps true happiness lies within?

34   People are more important than things

In 2007, Randy Pausch, an obscure 47-year-old academic with terminal pancreatic cancer and only months to live, became an overnight internet sensation. His 'Last Lecture' was viewed by over 18 million people on YouTube.

The 'Last Lecture' includes many wise insights consistent with Stoicism. Here's the Randy Pausch story that has stayed with me most:

One day Pausch proudly arrived at his sister's house in his brand-new convertible to take his young niece and nephew out for a spin. As they got into the car, his sister warned her children not to get Uncle Randy's new car dirty. As she talked, the children couldn't contain their laughter as they saw him deliberately pour soda all over the back seat!

I bet they still remember that moment with fondness, as well as the life lesson it taught them. You guessed it:

People are more important than things.

35   Keep the memories, not the clutter

From Kasey Pierce – editor of this book

I once knew a woman who was a bit of a hoarder. She was surrounded by a mess of clutter, and her personal life reflected it. The reason? She was so attached to these 'things' because they reminded her of the people who gave them to her, mostly deceased. I noticed she was also quite an unhappy person, uppity and anxious most of the time – needing to be in control of everything, even the uncontrollable. I always wanted to tell her that although these things reminded her of certain people, it seemed as if she valued the *things* more than the actual *memories*.

Desperately holding tight to suffocating clutter gifted to her wasn't bringing her loved ones back to life. In fact, these things were slowly taking *her life*.

36   The virtues – a check-in

The Stoics believe that while pursuing external things like pleasure, achievement and money doesn't provide a reliable path to true happiness, such a path does exist. The key is to develop certain *internal* qualities.

There are four internal qualities Stoics prize above all others – the four cardinal virtues, namely wisdom, courage, self-control and justice.

It's helpful to see each cardinal virtue as being at the heart of a family of related qualities:

Wisdom – knowledge, curiosity, creativity, insight, judgement and prudence

Courage – persistence, bravery, honesty, integrity, strength and determination

Self-control – self-discipline, self-regulation, temperance, patience and humility

Justice – fairness, kindness, teamwork, friendship, compassion and love

Spend a few moments rating yourself out of ten on each of the four cardinal virtues:

Wisdom

Courage

Self-control

Justice

37   Wisdom – the foundation of the virtues

Wisdom has a special place among the virtues. It is the key virtue required for all the other virtues.

The fifth-century BCE Athenian philosopher Socrates, as presented in the so-called Socratic dialogues of his pupil Plato, was an important influence on the ancient Stoics. In one of his dialogues, Plato has Socrates make the point about wisdom well in a conversation with Laches, a Greek general.

Socrates asks Laches to define courage.

'Remaining at one's post and fighting the enemy,' replies the general confidently.

Do you think that Socrates liked Laches' definition?

Can you think of any situations where standing firm might be foolhardy rather than courageous?

Socrates could. He reminded the general about a famous battle when the Spartans made a strategic withdrawal that ensured their victory. Would it have been courageous for the Spartans to stay at their posts – and lose? *No!* It would have been foolish. So, Socrates rejected Laches' definition of courage, because although fighting the enemy can at times be courageous, it depends on the context, on the bigger picture.

The same applies to every virtue. It might be unhelpful self-denial rather than self-control to refuse birthday cake. It might be imprudent rather than kind to give an abusive partner a second chance.

In each situation, the question to ask yourself is:

Given my understanding of the situation, is what I am proposing likely to be helpful or not, to me and others, in the long run, all things considered?

In other words, we need to exercise *good judgement*, which is part of the Stoic virtue of wisdom.

38   Money, money, money

The old ABBA classic suggests 'it's always sunny in a rich man's world'. However, what I think the big-haired Swedish pop sensations were really trying to say here was quite the opposite: money *doesn't* make you happy. Yet many people still do believe that if they become super-rich then – hey presto! – their lives will improve dramatically. Research on lottery winners suggests otherwise. After the initial rush of instant happiness, most winners tend to revert to their previous level of happiness. That's mainly because more money doesn't buy more wisdom.

Does money always make you happy? Indeed not ... There are many unhappy celebrities.

What do we call the quality that allows us to use money well? *Wisdom.*

39   Spot the virtue!

The Stoics suggested four qualities we need to develop to become virtuous – wisdom, courage, self-control and justice.

Name the virtue or virtues needed in each scenario.

1. Jeremy wants to talk to his boss about a pay rise.

2. Simon's doctor has advised him to cut out sugar.

3. Laura wants to decide whether to apply for a new job.

If you answered wisdom for all of them, then you can feel very pleased with yourself! The Stoics argue that the virtues are all connected and based on good judgement, which is part of wisdom. Most often, we need wisdom and at least one other virtue.

1. Jeremy needs wisdom to understand whether talking to his boss is courageous or foolish – he might then need courage to talk to his boss or self-control not to!

2. Simon needs wisdom to understand he needs self-control – and then self-control to follow up this insight.

3. Laura needs the wisdom and courage to make a change in her career.

How did you do?

40   Happiness comes from within

The Stoics think that you nail your colours to the wrong mast if you aim for goals like pleasure, achievement or material goods. They think that the virtues pave the way to lasting happiness and a good life.

Virtues are skills which enable you to both live well and be happy. Without them, you will make a mess of things in the long run – sometimes sooner!

Here is how the Stoic virtues can make you happier:

Courage allows you to handle fear well. Without courage, fear and discomfort may prevent you from doing things that are worthwhile and important.

Self-control enables you to manage your desires. Otherwise you will be prone to eat or drink the wrong things, cheat on your partner, or go astray in other ways that wreak havoc on your life.

Justice ensures you treat others well, exercising kindness and fairness. It creates and maintains not only harmony in relationships and community but harmony within.

Wisdom helps us to understand the world. While we can't control the whole world, we can control our perception of it – what's right or wrong, what is best for us all in the grand scheme of things, and what we can best do to bring that about.

The more you develop wisdom, the better your whole life will go.

41   You are not a sheep

'Do nothing like a sheep ... What then do we do as sheep? When we act gluttonously, lewdly, rashly, filthily, inconsiderately ... What have we lost? The rational faculty.'

Epictetus, *Discourses* 2.9

Pleasure and the absence of pain might well be a fitting goal for a sheep, but not for a human. We're a bit more complicated ... What is good for a sheep isn't necessarily good for a human being.

What *is* a fitting goal for you and me, then?

To develop and use our unique gift of rationality.

In other words, to develop wisdom and the other virtues. That's what the Stoics think.

Do you agree?

42   The V word!

Some people don't like the word 'virtue'.

It does have old-fashioned and preachy overtones, certainly. However, forget visions of Queen Victoria and not having any fun. The virtues are simply qualities that help us live both good and happy lives.

How so?

The Greek word for virtue, *arete*, means 'excellence'. So, by becoming virtuous you become an excellent human being. Or, as Modern Stoic Larry Becker (2017) puts it, you become a 'virtuoso at living'.

So next time someone asks you why you are reading a book on Stoicism, just tell them you want to lead a better and happier life.

Or, if you feel daring, tell them you're training to become a virtuoso at living …

43   Character strengths

Contemporary psychologists have begun to take a strong interest in measuring the virtues. The best-known measure is the Values in Action (VIA) classification of character strengths. This lists 24 character strengths grouped into six virtues.

Take the VIA survey today at https://www.viacharacter.org/ (it's free).

What are your top character strengths?

How can you use them more today?

44   Extend the use of your 'top' virtue today

The path to true happiness is to develop and use *all* the virtues. Many people find it easiest, though, to start with their top virtue – the one they score highest on, because it's the quality that is already well developed.

Here are some examples of how people have extended their use of their top virtue:

- Lucy scored highest on *courage*. She already speaks up at work but has shied from confronting her teenage child about tidying their room. She resolves to do that as her Stoic challenge today.

- Miranda's top virtue is *justice*. Though she is usually very fair and kind, she has been holding a grudge over a criticism a colleague made at work. Perhaps, on reflection, the colleague had a point … She decides to forgive and forget, lightening her emotional load and ultimately freeing herself of irrational and crippling feelings that serve no one.

- Bob's top virtue is *wisdom*. He usually reads one entry from this book each day, so today he decides to read two entries instead! (Yes, we know there are lots of other ways of developing ways of wisdom besides reading this book …)

How can you use your top virtue in an extra way today?

45   The unity of the virtues

You clearly need wisdom to have the other virtues, because you need good judgement to tell the difference between, for example, courage and rashness or self-control and unhelpful self-denial.

But can you be *wise* without being *courageous*? Can you be *courageous* without being *just*?

'No,' answer the Stoics.

Consider Ethan and Raj, a married couple.

Raj is thinking about quitting his job. He thinks of this in terms of his needing to be courageous. 'I need the courage to quit my job,' he tells his friends. But how can he know whether this is true courage unless he also possesses justice – the knowledge of whether quitting would be fair to Ethan?

Stoics call this idea the *unity of the virtues*.

In practice, it means that you shouldn't try to cultivate *just* one virtue – you need all of them!

Today, look out for opportunities to practise each of the four main, or cardinal, virtues – *wisdom*, *courage*, *justice* and *self-control*.

46   A five-minute meditation to start your day

Of course, you'll have a strong desire to master each virtue. However, this full-speed-ahead approach is much like trying to carry all the grocery bags into the house in one trip: putting unnecessary strain on yourself and becoming so overwhelmed that you may just drop everything. Longevity in the application of each virtue takes practice.

Here is one of my favourite ways to develop a specific virtue.

At the start of the day, write down the name of one virtue that you want to work on today.

Sam writes down 'courage'.

Next, close your eyes and identify various opportunities you might have to use that virtue today.

Sam runs through his day and picks several likely times when he can show courage – such as giving difficult but constructive feedback to a colleague.

Open your eyes and jot down the opportunities you have thought of. Read it through, twice.

Sam writes down the situations when courage is likely to be handy. He reads his list so he is more likely to remember to use courage when he needs it later in the day.

What virtue do you want to work on today?

47   An evening review

Another good way to develop a specific virtue is to spend five minutes at the end of the day reviewing it. It's great to combine this with the morning meditation on the same virtue (see 46).

Here Sam is reviewing how well he did on his courage challenge:

> What went well: *I gave the constructive feedback – and there was no problem. I also went to the gym, even though I feel a bit self-conscious there.*

> What I could do better: *I guess I could have spent longer on some exercises at the gym – I can do that tomorrow.*

> What I omitted to do: *I've only just thought about this now. I fell out with my brother around Christmas time, and it's time to patch things up. That will take courage. It's important though, so I will send a text right now.*

This evening, spend five minutes reviewing how you got on with a specific virtue:

- ■ What went well
- ■ What I could do better
- ■ What I omitted to do

48   Does virtue pay?

Stoics think that you shouldn't be virtuous for the wrong reason. Virtue, they believe, is its own reward. Nevertheless, you may be interested to learn that recent research strongly suggests that virtue *does* pay.

Here are some of the most interesting findings:

- Steger, Kashdan and Oishi (2008) found that doing things in line with virtue (such as expressing gratitude, volunteering and persevering in a valued goal even in the face of obstacles) was associated with higher well-being than things that were not (casual sex, buying things for yourself and getting drunk).
- Park, Peterson and Seligman (2004) found that all the 24 VIA character strengths were associated with life satisfaction. Curiosity, love, hope, zest and gratitude showed the strongest link.
- Emmons (2003) found that values associated with work, intimacy, spirituality and transcendence (going beyond your own self-interest) had a positive relationship with well-being and purpose, while other values connected with power, money, status and attractiveness did not.

So, whether you think of virtue as being its own reward, or whether you're interested in the consequences of being virtuous, the moral is clear.

Follow virtue.

49   Is feeling good all there is to 'the good life'?

Imagine you must make this choice, right now:

You can continue your current life, or you can choose to plug permanently into a virtual-reality machine. If you choose to be plugged in, you won't know it's not reality. It's absolutely guaranteed that while plugged into the machine you will feel great, for the rest of your life.

There's a catch, though ... A week or two in this virtual-reality pleasure machine isn't an option. You have a stark choice: stay in the real world or plug into the pleasure machine until you die.

Would you plug in?

Most people answer 'no'. They give reasons such as:

'My experiences would be fake.'

'My life would be a waste.'

'I wouldn't grow as a person.'

'I wouldn't really be there for the people I care about.'

But you sure would feel good!

Does this mean that there is more to true happiness than just feeling good ...?

50   Not such a merry-go-round

'Pleasure dies at the very moment when it charms us most ... it soon cloys and wearies us, and fades away as soon as its first impulse is over.'
Seneca, *On the Happy Life* 7.3

I went to collect my shiny new car! How happy I felt! I imagined the admiring looks I would get from friends and neighbours!

A few weeks later and the novelty had worn off, just like the gloss on the bonnet. Friends and neighbours had been surprisingly uninterested in my new purchase. Very soon, my happiness returned to its previous level.

And that, according to the Stoics, is one of the problems with pursuing the life of pleasure. We just go round in a circle, like a hamster on a wheel: Hunger ... pursuit ... fleeting pleasure ... more hunger ... more pursuit ...

These days psychologists call this the 'hedonic treadmill'. But Seneca and the Stoics knew about the futility of the pursuit of pleasure a long time ago.

Today, notice how fleeting your pleasures are.

51   The joy of Stoicism

While they are opposed to the pursuit of unethical pleasures, Stoics are no killjoys.

In fact, 'joy' is one of the three encouraged Stoic emotions. What's more, in our research we've found a very strong link between Stoicism and positive emotions such as contentment and optimism. One of the most striking findings in ten years of research is that zest turns out to be the character strength most associated with Stoicism and most enhanced by the practice of it.

What's zest? It's what the A. A. Milne character Tigger epitomizes: that feeling you get when you wake up full of beans and looking forward to the day ahead.

How is it that Stoics are so joyful and full of zest?

Since you're not trying to control the uncontrollable, you don't set yourself up for disappointments that could turn you into an Eeyore.

What's more, when you do the right thing, you get positive, enduring and zestful feelings – rather than the spikes you get from sensory pleasure.

That's the joy of Stoicism.

52   Notice your positive qualities

Right now, spend a few moments recalling a time in the last 24 hours when you have used a virtue, in however small a way. Identify which virtue or virtues you used.

Susie recalls how she listened considerately to her housemate's romantic problems. (*kindness* and *justice*)

Harry remembers how he went for a run, even though he didn't feel like doing so. (*courage*)

Ray thinks about how he didn't buy so much alcohol when he went shopping. (*moderation*)

How does recalling your own use of a virtue make you feel?

53   No shortcut to happiness

Have you ever seen the movie *GoodFellas*? At first, the gangsters in the film seem to have found a shortcut to happiness. They get the girls, drive fast cars, and never have to wait in line. Yet, by the end of the film, they all wound up with broken relationships, in jail, or dead.

It's not so hard to see that their happiness isn't likely to last. If (spoiler alert!) you cheat, shoot people who irritate you, double-cross and rob banks, then at some point your misbehaviour is quite likely to catch up with you.

It's a further step to understanding that the gangsters suffer because they lack the very qualities advocated by the Stoic virtues. The 'goodfellas' lack self-control, justice and a moral sense. It's because of this that their happiness is not sustainable.

But here's a thought: Could it be that the gangsters are just an exaggerated version of all of us?

Don't we all do things that seem to benefit us in the short term but harm us when we look at the big picture? Like when we eat that unhealthy cake or gossip about a friend?

What shortcuts to happiness do you attempt?

54 Mushrooms, toadstools and the dichotomy of value

I was out walking the other day in a forest with lots of mushrooms and toadstools and it got me thinking about Stoicism.

I can hear your complaint straightaway:

It doesn't take much to get you thinking about Stoicism! What have fungi got to do with Stoicism?

Bear with me. Would you be happy if next time you went to the supermarket, they had started labelling mushrooms as fungi?

I'd be a bit worried that it might be a toadstool and not a mushroom!

Exactly. It would put you in a lot of jeopardy.

And your point?

Well, the Stoics think that this is how it stands with *all* the usual things we think of as being good, not just fungi. For example, money is good for you if you spend it on education or healthy food, bad if you spend it on unhealthy food or drugs.

That's true, so what should we do?

We need to withhold judgement about whether things like money are really good. The only things we can label as unconditionally good are the qualities that enable us to tell the difference.

And I guess these would be none other than the virtues?

Exactly. My Modern Stoic colleague Chris Gill refers to this as the *dichotomy of value*. Just as there is a dichotomy in the world of

> fungi – between edible mushrooms and poisonous toadstools – so there is with everything.
>
> *So, the virtues are unconditionally good and everything else is to be treated with caution.*
>
> Precisely.
>
> *So the most important thing is for us to develop these qualities, the virtues.*

What toxic outcomes can the dichotomy of value help you avoid today?

55 Freya's frustrations

Freya has learned that her colleague Marie has just got the promotion that she expected for herself. Her initial response is understandable but, frankly, not too Stoic. 'It's not fair. Life sucks. Maybe I should quit. And I'm definitely not going out for drinks with Marie and the gang tomorrow.'

How could the dichotomy of value – *Things like money and status may be of some value, but the virtues are of greater value* – help her deal with the situation?

Jot down your answer before you proceed.

56 Freya uses the dichotomy of value

This is how Freya uses the dichotomy of value to respond well to being passed over for promotion:

Extra money and recognition are valuable but would they really make me happy? I have enough money already, to be honest. Status is nice – but do I want to be defined by what other people think of me?

A little voice says: *But what about fairness? This just isn't fair.*

How do I know it isn't fair? I don't really know how well suited Marie is to this role. She may be a better option. But I do want to advance my career and understand why I was passed over.

So, what virtues do I need here?

All of them – self-control, courage, justice and wisdom:

Self-control – to control myself so I don't just lash out and act on impulse.

Courage – to have a chat with my boss about why I didn't get the promotion and what I need to do to get it next time.

Justice – it's not Marie's fault that she got promoted! I can try to be happy for her. Gosh, this is actually an opportunity for me to rise above my instinctive reaction and be a better version of myself!

Wisdom – it's much wiser to see whether I can progress my career in this company than to quit on impulse just because I feel robbed. It's also wisdom that helps me understand the dichotomy of value and to realise which virtues to apply.

Can you use Freya's example to become a better version of yourself?

57   Preferred indifferents

At some point in your Stoic journey, you are bound to come across the phrase 'preferred indifferents'. It's another name for external goods, like status, money and pleasure, though it's a confusing phrase. How can you be indifferent to something if you prefer it? And should you be indifferent to things like the health and the well-being of your loved ones?

In fact, Stoics are *not* indifferent to the indifferents. There are some things that we naturally pursue, and as long as we obtain them in a virtuous way, that's fine.

It's natural to prefer health to ill-health and having money to living in poverty. External goods are called 'indifferent' not because we should be indifferent to them but because they do not *make the difference* between true happiness and misery, between a good life and a bad life.

The virtues are the only sure path to true happiness, the only things that are unconditionally good.

58   Happiness is within your grasp

To paraphrase Marcus Aurelius (*Meditations* 6.51), there are three types of people: people who think happiness is all about praise, people who think it's all about pleasure, and people who think it's all about their own actions. Marcus believes that it is this last group of people who are wisest.

If you depend on other people's approval or make feeling good your main value, then happiness is outside your control.

If, on the other hand, you follow the wise and make your own virtuous actions your main goal in life, happiness is very much within your grasp.

Why?

Because you can always, like the Stoic Archer (see **12**), try to do the right thing.

And that's enough.

59   Can you think of anything better?

In his *Meditations 3.6*, Marcus Aurelius poses this challenge:

> 'If you can find anything in human life better than justice, truthfulness, self-control, and courage [...] turn to it with all your heart and enjoy the supreme good that you have found.'
>
> *Meditations* 3.6

Can you think of anything better than the virtues as the path towards true happiness?

Or do you find yourself in agreement with the 'last good emperor'?

60 Make yourself beautiful

> 'See what Socrates says to Alcibiades, most beautiful
> and charming of men: "Strive then to attain beauty."
> What does he say to him? Does he say, "Arrange your
> hair and smooth your legs"? God forbid! But "Set your
> will in order, rid it of bad judgements."'
>
> Epictetus, *Discourses* 3.1

When Socrates told Alcibiades to make himself beautiful, he wasn't recommending a trip to the salon. He was talking about inner beauty.

Time is unkind to the flesh no matter how many products we invest in. Better to invest in the internal, the impression you'll leave this world, for that is eternal.

Follow-up

■ Retake the quiz in **31** and the check-in in **36** to assess your progress.

■ The essential entry in this chapter is **40**: Happiness comes from within.

■ Decide which of the practical exercises – **46, 47** and **52** – works best for you.

CHAPTER 3
STOIC SERENITY

This chapter will introduce you to key Stoic ideas that can help you keep your cool, even in the most trying times. Everyone experiences emotional upsets. But it's important to maintain a level of Stoic emotional awareness so that you can identify emotions that are just that, emotions, and not a reflection of actual reality – although it may seem that way in the moment! It's important because, if we always accept our initial impressions, it could cause us to say or do things we can never take back, resulting, for example, in the loss of a friendship, job or marriage.

In this chapter, you will be introduced to four central thinking traps that cause emotional upsets and how to detect and avoid them. You'll also discover which sentence in Epictetus's *Handbook* launched a revolution in the treatment of psychological problems. You'll hear the stories of seasoned Stoics and how Stoicism helped them handle some really tricky situations without losing their composure. Finally, I'll be rounding things off by giving you a five-step framework to set your own path to Stoic serenity. So, keep calm and carry on reading!

61   Emotional check-in

Let's start with a quick check-in.

Over the last week, how often have you felt the following emotions? For each, write down a value 0–4 where 0 = Never; 1 = Occasionally; 2 = Sometimes; 3 = Often; and 4 = A lot.

a. irritated, frustrated or angry

b. anxious, panicky or worried

c. depressed, low or down

d. guilty, embarrassed or ashamed

e. upset, distressed or troubled

Now add up your scores. Your score will lie between 0 (achieved Stoic serenity) to 20 (lacking serenity).

Your score at the start of the chapter is …

62   How you think affects how you feel

Over half a century ago, psychotherapists Albert Ellis and Tim Beck were becoming increasingly frustrated with Freudian psychoanalysis. So many hours spent trawling through their patients' life stories, so little improvement. Could there be a more direct and efficient way to help their patients?

Stumbling upon Epictetus's *Handbook*, they read this sentence:

> 'People are disturbed not by things, but by the views
> which they take of them.'

If that's true, we can feel better by becoming more aware of how we are upsetting ourselves and learning how to think differently.

In time, Beck and Ellis developed their own therapies based on this central Stoic idea, and these have become known as cognitive behavioural therapy (CBT) and rational emotive behaviour therapy (REBT). Countless people have been helped by these therapies since.

Whenever you feel upset, try to detect the part you play in that happening.

63   The power to choose how to feel

We've all been there …

It's been hours and your partner still hasn't replied to your text, or you may have felt intentionally left out of a gathering with your friends.

Of course, it's natural for these things to make you feel irritated or angry, but what if you gave the benefit of the doubt to the people in this situation? Would you then go from feeling irritated and angry to feeling much calmer? Would you become a more compassionate person if you simply considered that perhaps these people were preoccupied or simply weren't thinking?

How much does your desire for peace, love and understanding outweigh your desire to want to feel angry and bitter? *The choice is yours.*

64 Observe your thoughts and emotions – keep a journal

> 'Those who do not observe the movements of their
> own minds must of necessity be unhappy.'
>
> Marcus Aurelius, *Meditations* 2.8

Marcus Aurelius knew that we need to be proactive to keep on top of our emotions. That's why he kept his journal, which has come down to us as his *Meditations*.

Josh is a 22-year-old who has just finished university. He's delighted to have found his first job but has to live at home again, with a three-hour daily commute. Josh is becoming increasingly frustrated.

This is what he writes in his first journal entry:

Feeling exhausted and quite low about my daily commute. I can't go on like this!

Josh found this a helpful first step, allowing him some detachment from the situation. In a flash of insight, Josh understood that he must move closer to work. As he gained clarity, it was like a dark cloud had lifted. His very first Stoic journal entry helped him realize that it was within his power to change things. This solution might appear obvious, but being caught up in frustration clouds your vision.

Today, jot down your emotions and the thoughts that are associated with them.

65   Picture yourself as a comic-book hero!

How are you doing on your Stoic journal?

Some people, like Josh, find it easy to identify the thoughts upsetting them. Others may find it harder to put their finger on what exactly is causing them distress. If you're one of those people, you're not alone.

Imagine, however, that you're a comic-book hero.* Better yet, imagine you're Spiderman and your 'Spidey-sense' is tingling. What would your thought bubble say? Would you be able to identify what's triggering *your* Spidey-sense?

Try to put your thoughts into words today by using this exercise.

66   Stoic serenity is as easy as ABCD

Over the next dozen entries, you'll learn about the four main ways that your thoughts can cause negative emotions, according to Stoicism.

You can make progress right away by learning them – and it's as easy as ABCD.

Assumptions – are you making a snap judgement or assuming too much?

Blame – are you blaming others or yourself?

Catastrophizing – are you thinking something is worse than it really is?

Dichotomies – are you neglecting the dichotomies of control or value?

Just be mindful that shooting webs may be frowned upon at the office!

Today's Stoic challenge is to learn your ABCD – spend a few moments learning what each letter stands for. I promise it will be worth the effort!

67   Avoid snap judgements

If you are human, then you're probably an Olympic champion at making snap judgements. Do you find yourself thinking things like:

'He is ignoring me'

'They are going to be cross with me'?

Do you agree that if you buy into these snap judgements, you are bound to feel upset?

However, you don't have to accept these snap judgements as if they were solid facts. Are any of the above judgements the only explanation for what happened?

'He is ignoring me.' *Maybe he's preoccupied.*

'They are going to be cross with me.' *Is that a fact or just my fear?*

As the old saying goes, 'ASSUME and you make an ASS out of U and ME.'

Today, be mindful of snap judgements.

68 'That's just my initial impression'

'More things frighten us than really hurt us.'

Seneca, *Letters* 13.4

If snap judgements are likely to make an ass of us all, what can we do about it? It's hard to stop judging! That's what we humans are wired to do. But we can train ourselves to be more mindful that we are making snap judgements.

Here's one way:

When an upsetting thought enters your mind, the first thing to do is remind yourself it's just an impression in your mind and not the thing it claims to represent.

Or how about saying these mantras to yourself whenever you are upset?

'That's just my initial impression.'

'I feel this way, but that doesn't make it true.'

'A thought is not a fact, it's just an opinion.'

Try each of them on for size and see which one works best.

69   The passport control officer

> 'We ought not to accept an appearance without examination, but we should say, "Wait, let me see what you are and from where you come", like the night-watch says, "Show me your pass."'
>
> Epictetus, *Discourses* 3.12.14–15

At passport control, they take care not to let *anyone* potentially dangerous into the country. They take a good look at your photo and then at you to check that you are who you claim to be. Epictetus advises us to do the same thing with our initial thoughts.

Passport control has a big responsibility – not to let in the wrong people.

You have an equal responsibility – not to let in snap judgements.

Today, think of yourself as passport control to guard against snap judgements.

70   Accept what you can't control

> 'If something concerns anything not in our control, be prepared to say that it is nothing to you.'
>
> Epictetus, *Handbook* 1

One part of the Stoic way is to take control when we can. With Josh (see **64**) it meant moving out. But what about times when we have no control?

If you can't take control of external things, you can always take control of how you think about them.

Epictetus suggests we say this about all the things we cannot control: 'It is nothing to me!' Could this work for you? Here are two similar phrases that my clients have found helpful:

'I can't change it, so I'm not going to let it bother me.'

'I've done all I can, so there's no point thinking about it. Move on!'

Which do you prefer?

71   No use crying over spilt milk

Victoria tried out two versions of yesterday's mantra. Here is her feedback:

'It was sooo liberating! My ex posted something on Facebook about his new relationship. It is nothing to do with me and I shouldn't take it personally.

'Later, I spilt coffee over my top. I can't change that, but I can change my top!

'Hey, I've just remembered a saying of my nan's: "There's no use crying over spilt milk." I wonder if she was a Stoic without knowing it ...'

72   The genius of Seneca

You're driving along without a care in the world. Suddenly a car pulls out in front of you. Your reaction may be to slam on the brakes, muttering, 'What the ...? That idiot might have killed me!'

Seneca's genius was to understand that this is an automatic response. It's the fight/flight response. But it doesn't have to dictate what you do next.

What happens if you don't challenge your snap judgement? Worst-case scenario – road rage!

Or – and this is the Stoic way – you take a few breaths to calm down and remind yourself that no one has died.

You can choose to fuel the flames or to put the fire out.

Today, notice initial, automatic responses.

73   Stoicism under fire

From Eve Riches – mentor, psychology teacher and Stoic educator who is registered blind / severely sight-impaired

I was at a busy train station when a man ripped my guide dog's lead out of my hands and tried to steal him. I was screaming for help and shouted for the police, who eventually arrived.

Shaking, I worried that this was the end of my travelling independently. I realized, though, that while I was not in control of what happened, I still had a choice in how to react.

I was angry until I thought about the kind of life someone must be living to steal a guide dog. He is a fellow human, worthy of compassion. Anger was going to do *me* more harm. The event left me feeling more trust in my character. I now realize that I can trust myself to act with wisdom even in an emergency.

74   It's only money …

Quick quiz: The *dichotomy of value* is defined as …

a. The difference between what things cost on Black Fridays and the rest of the time.

b. Doing the right thing, with virtue, is the only thing that is really good. External things like money, status and pleasure are of less value.

c. No idea, it's all Greek to me!

As you may remember from Chapter 2, the dichotomy of value means that doing the right thing, with virtue, is the only thing that is really good and so everything else becomes less important.

Someone just dropped your favourite mug.

Ask yourself: *Does my happiness really depend on this mug?*

It's in your power to wipe out the judgement that external things matter so much.

75   Stoicism on the road

From Dr Keith Seddon – author of *Stoic Serenity and Epictetus' Handbook* and *The Tablet of Cebes: Guides to Stoic Living*

Moving to a new house last year, over two hundred miles away, required travelling to the other end of the country, there and back, round and round in endless repetition, a total distance of over 2,000 miles.

Through all this toil I reminded myself, as had Marcus Aurelius in his *Meditations*, that I would be confronted by rudeness, incompetence and travails of all sorts. I must not hand over my equanimity to others.

To me, things were neither good nor bad, but merely preferred or dispreferred, lacking any power to perturb. I remember one afternoon, creeping along for ages in third gear behind a tractor, thinking: 'This delay simply does not matter. Events will unfold at the rate Zeus has set: all I have to do is drive safely with my equanimity intact.'

76   Everything has two handles

'Everything has two handles: one by which it may be carried, another by which it cannot.'

Epictetus, *Handbook* 43

Things don't have the power to make you upset.

You have the power to stop them upsetting you.

We all have this superpower – our inner Epictetus!

The next time something difficult happens to you, simply remind yourself that there are two ways you can handle it – and choose the better way.

77   My inner Epictetus

From Chuck Chakrapani – founder of TheStoicGym.com, editor of *THE STOIC* and author of many books

I was having dinner on a restaurant patio in Athens when I placed my wallet and iPhone on the table. A young boy walked in and showed me a paper with something written on it. I politely asked him to go away. He walked out with his paper and my iPhone and wallet – which his paper had hidden so he could grab them!

Naturally, I was upset. Then I heard my inner Epictetus speak up. His voice was particularly clear and authoritative on this occasion because we had spent the day before walking in his footsteps among the ruins of Nicopolis.

'Didn't I tell you that every situation has two handles?'

I was using a handle powered by frustration. What was the other handle? To be compassionate.

Would I exchange places with the thief? I realized I am better off than him even without my things. My problems were trivial compared to his.

Epictetus always comes through for me! And I'm happy to report this is true even when I'm not in Greece.

78   The power of the four virtues

> 'When anything happens to you, always remember to turn
> to yourself and ask what power you have to deal with it.'
>
> Epictetus, *Handbook* 10

The Stoics think that a *great* way to handle any situation is to look through the lens of the four main virtues.

The other day I had trouble sleeping because I was having second thoughts about a pension I had been talked into. Then I remembered the four virtues. Could I feel less disturbed if I looked at my situation through this lens?

I started with self-control:

'I will postpone thinking about it until tomorrow when I can think about it rationally.'

This helped me get to sleep. Come my morning walk, I was able to view the situation logically, taking each virtue in turn:

Wisdom – I need to find out more – tonight.

Justice – I need to be fair to everyone.

Courage – If I need to renegotiate or withdraw from the agreement.

Wisdom (again) – It's only money!

Feeling so much more in control, the virtues turned out to be my superpower.

How can looking at a situation through the lens of the four main virtues help you today?

79 Take the 'View from Above'

My parents loved telling me how much better everything was in their day. They praised to high heaven a radio programme called *The Brains Trust*, especially one regular panellist, Bertrand Russell. 'He's always so wise and calm,' enthused my mother.

What she didn't know was that Russell had once been tormented by the idea of public speaking. He used to hope he would break his leg to avoid having to make a speech! Then he asked himself one key question:

'How much will it matter, from the point of view of the whole universe, whether I speak well or badly?'

Russell realized that the universe would remain much the same in either case. The less he cared about how well he spoke, the better he spoke. He learned this idea from his reading of the Stoics and the technique known as the 'View from Above'.

Can the View from Above help you overcome one of *your* fears?

80 How much will this matter a year from now?

I too can catastrophize, and the 'View from Above' has come to my assistance on many occasions.

One time I was worried about getting a speeding ticket. I recalled Bertrand Russell and how, from the point of view of the universe, my getting a speeding ticket didn't matter one iota. I continued by asking myself this related question:

'On a scale of 0–100, of all the bad things that might happen in your life, how bad a catastrophe would this be?'

Of course, getting a speeding ticket hardly registered in terms of possible catastrophes that might befall me.

Another time, I was cross because I'd broken an expensive pair of ear buds. This time, I asked myself a different question:

'How much will this matter to me in a year's time?'

'Not one jot!' came the reply.

> How much does it matter from the point of view of the universe?
>
> How bad is this, really?
>
> How much will this matter a year from now?

Which View from Above do you want to try?

81   Don't play the blame game

> 'To accuse others for one's own misfortunes is a sign
> of want of education; to accuse oneself shows that one's
> education has begun; to accuse neither oneself nor others
> shows that one's education is complete.'
>
> Epictetus, *Handbook* 5

You wake up late for breakfast and rush downstairs. As you open the fridge, yoghurt spills out all over. You leave home in a foul mood, made worse by getting stuck in heavy traffic. You arrive late for work, ready to find fault with everything and everyone there.

Is it just me, or do you too find that when things go wrong, it's all too easy to start on the slippery slope of blaming everyone?

'Why did they put the yoghurt *there*?'

Or maybe you are the type of person who tends to blame themselves?

'Why am I so clumsy?'

But think … *Does blaming yourself or others do any good? Or does it just make things worse?*

What would be a better approach?

82   Stoic forgiveness

From John Harlow – Stoic Survival Facilitator

Climbing vertically up a rope out of one of Britain's deepest caves, I found another party had accidentally pulled up my rope, leaving my partner and me stranded 50 metres below the surface. Waiting for rescue in miserable conditions, I found comfort in Stoicism. We considered what a good and helpful reaction might look like in our situation and avoided casting judgements on our sensations of hunger and cold. That simple reflection certainly helped during our 12-hour wait for rescue in the mud. Once out, however, Stoicism helped me to forgive the individual who had pulled up our rope. He was deeply sorry for his mistake and determined to ensure it never happened again. Without Stoicism, I might have judged his past actions and not his character.

83   Blame no one

> 'If someone goes wrong, instruct them kindly
> and point out what is being overlooked; if you can't,
> blame yourself or, better, not even yourself.'

Marcus Aurelius, *Meditations* 10.4

When you blame other people, you get sucked into an endless cycle of negativity. You blame them, they blame you, and it all turns very ugly. 'An eye for an eye and the whole world is blind,' as a wise man once said.

As Marcus points out, it's possible to correct someone tactfully. Humour is one way to defuse potentially delicate situations.

If your partner or housemate has placed the yoghurt pot inexpertly, how about 'Those yoghurt pots are lethal! How can we stop them attacking us!' rather than 'You idiot, why did you leave the yoghurt there?!'

If John Harlow could avoid the blame game when he was stuck in one of Britain's deepest caves, surely we can avoid it in our everyday melodramas.

84   Quiz: the four biggest thinking traps

Remember back at 66 when I promised that Stoic serenity would be as easy as ABCD? Now that we have looked at examples of each of these, it's time for a quick quiz. Without reading ahead, what does each letter stand for?

Yes, that's right, it was:

Assumptions – are you making a snap judgement or assuming too much?

Blame – are you blaming others or yourself?

Catastrophizing – are you thinking something is worse than it really is?

Dichotomies – forgetting about these dichotomies:
Control – getting bothered about things you can't control
Value – overvaluing external things like money, pleasure and status
Response – choosing the wrong handle.

Today's Stoic challenge is to notice yourself falling foul of a Stoic thinking trap. *Knowledge is power!*

85   Dealing with sadness and anxiety

Chloe looks on Facebook and sees that her friends are going out to the pub and haven't invited her. She feels sad and anxious. Chloe realizes that these are the thoughts that are upsetting her: 'That's awful. They don't want me as a friend.'

Pick two Stoic thinking traps from the list in 84 that you think most apply.

What did you answer? I answered:

Dichotomies:

Control – *'It's happened and its pointless trying to control what other people have done.'*

Value – *'What my friends think need not define me.'*

Assumptions – *'I don't really have any evidence that they don't want me as a friend. I did tell them how busy I was.'*

Today's Stoic challenge is to work in a similar way on something that has happened to you in the last 24 hours.

86   Managing guilt

Maisie feels guilty when she arrives late to pick up her daughter Annie from her nursery school. She thinks: 'I'm a lousy mother. I can't even do a simple thing like pick up my daughter on time.'

Pick two Stoic thinking traps that apply to Maisie.

What did you answer? I answered:

Catastrophizing – being late doesn't make her a lousy mother.

Blaming herself – that's not going to help; it would be better to think of how she can do better next time.

You could also have mentioned the dichotomy of control – no point crying over spilt milk!

Today, be on the lookout for thinking traps and *catch them happening in real time, before they have any real impact.*

87   Real-time serenity – stop and take a time out

'Between stimulus and response there is a space. In that space is our power to choose our response. In our response lies our growth and our freedom.' Stephen Covey wrote these words in his multi-million-selling *The 7 Habits of Highly Effective People*. Covey couldn't recall the original author (it wasn't Viktor Frankl, as the internet would have you believe!), but I'd put good money on them being inspired by Stoicism.

To put these wise words into practice, I suggest these two steps:

1. *Stop*. When you are upset, notice that you are upset and pause.
2. *Time out*. Use that space between the stimulus and your response to decide what to do next.

88   Five STOIC steps to Stoic serenity

Did you notice that the two tips from yesterday, Stop and Time out, are the first two letters in the word STOIC? In fact, the word STOIC spells out my entire framework for attaining Stoic serenity in real time.

Stop – notice when you are starting to get upset.

Time out – take a breath and make some time to analyse the situation.

Observe – your initial impressions and snap judgements.

Identify which of the four Stoic thinking traps apply.

Choose how to handle the situation Stoically.

Today's task is simple. Learn what the acronym STOIC stands for. Tomorrow, we will see how Maisie, the guilty mum, puts it into action!

89 Maisie starts to become more STOIC ...

Remember Maisie from 86, the mum who felt guilty? Since then, the nursery has instigated fines for any parents who turn up late!

Yesterday, once again Maisie struggled to leave work on time, and then she couldn't find a parking spot and had to park a few minutes away. She used this walking time to become more STOIC.

S – Stop – *'I'm in a state right now and need to calm down.'*

T – Time out – *'OK, I've got three minutes – I can take a deep breath and think.'*

O – Observe – *'Well, I'm annoyed at getting fined. I'm anxious that I'll be judged for being a bad mum. I feel guilty that Annie will be there on her own, crying!'*

Can you help Maisie with the next steps – identifying thinking traps and choosing a response? The answers are in the next entry.

90 Maisie becomes more STOIC!

This is how Maisie completed the STOIC framework:

I – Identify Stoic thinking traps:

Assumptions – Annie may be enjoying herself. I have no idea what the nursery workers are really thinking.

Blame – No point blaming myself, but I can think about how I can do things better tomorrow.

Catastrophizing – The fine isn't a lot of money, and it's only money.

Dichotomies – I can't *control* that I am late today. I can control how I respond and what I do tomorrow.

– I shouldn't *value* money or what other people think so much as my character.

C – Choose a Stoic response. *'I feel much calmer! The above tells me exactly how to respond, and it all makes sense.'*

How do you feel about the way Maisie handled it?

Follow-up

■ It's time to check by retaking the quiz in **61**. How do your scores compare?

■ The essential entries here are **89** and **90**, which together describe the STOIC framework, which pulls together many of the ideas in this chapter.

■ Try out the STOIC framework regularly as well as some of the other practical exercises. If anger and frustration remain an issue, further help is at hand in Chapter 10.

CHAPTER 4
FINDING THE RIGHT DIRECTION

At Socrates' trial for impiety in 399 BCE, Plato records the older philosopher as saying: 'The unexamined life is not worth living.'

Reflecting on your values and life goals is a great way to begin examining your own life. Your life goals act as a compass, telling you whether you're heading in the right direction or not.

If you were to work with a life coach, that's probably where they would start. Socrates, were he your personal mentor, would go further and ask searching questions to establish whether they were the right life goals for you. Questions like, 'Do you feel your compass is leading you in the right direction?'

Epictetus would add some very Stoic questions such as, 'Are goals within your control?' and 'Will they help you fulfil your key roles and contribute to the common good?'

This chapter will help you define, refine and work towards your life goals. It's like having your own Stoic life coaching session!

91 Define your life goals

> 'If you do not know to which port you are sailing,
> no wind is favourable.'
>
> Seneca, *Letters* 71.3

Do you have a clear idea of your direction in life? Some do. They would say: 'I want to be a good parent' or 'I'm going to be a successful entrepreneur'.

Most of us lack such clarity. Philosophical exercises – mind gym – can give us more clarity. Here's one of my favourite thought experiments.

Imagine that a genie materializes and makes this offer: 'Tell me your vision of your good life and I will make it happen.'

You can have a list of up to five ingredients that will make your good life. What would be on your list? Write them here:

1. _____

2. _____

3. _____

4. _____

5. _____

92   Emily's life goals

Emily is a 36-year-old working mother with two young children. She isn't unhappy, yet life could be better … Her children have started to call her 'grumpy mummy'.

Emily quickly jots down her top four life goals:

1. Be a good mother, partner and daughter.

2. Have a successful career.

3. Leave the world a slightly better place.

4. Enjoy good friendships.

Emily thinks about what her fifth goal should be. As a budding Stoic, she writes:

5. Develop my character so I become the best version of me.

What advice would you give Emily to help her work towards these five goals?

93 Just do the right thing!

Identifying your life goals is a fantastic first step. Sometimes, as the advertising slogan says, you can *just do it!*

Emily wants to leave the world a slightly better place. She asks herself if there's anything she can do about that right *now*.

She suddenly realizes that she hasn't seen her elderly neighbour for some time. When Emily checks in on her, it turns out she's in poor health. Emily decides to do some of her grocery shopping to help her out.

Just a small act of kindness can make a big difference.

What can you do to follow through *your* life goals (see **91**)?

94 My early midlife crisis

> 'We should not, like sheep, follow the flock that has gone
> before us, and thus proceed not where we ought,
> but where the rest are going.'
>
> Seneca, *On the Happy Life* 1.1

I was reasonably happy in my twenties. I had a good job in IT and good friends. We worked hard and enjoyed life. But as I approached 30, I had an early midlife crisis – yes, there is such a thing!

I detected a pattern. The clients kept changing their minds about their requirements. Four projects in a row got canned. All that work for nothing!

A thought crept into my head: 'I'm going to spend 80,000 hours of my life at work. What difference is that going to make to anyone?' 'Not much,' came the reply.

Seneca's words rang in my ears. What port was I sailing towards? Should I follow the herd?

Where is *your* life heading? Is it a path you should follow?

95 Step-by-step planning to work towards a life goal

'A journey of a thousand miles begins with a single step.'

Lao Tzu

Sometimes getting what we need is simple; sometimes not. When I had my early midlife crisis, I couldn't just snap my fingers for a more meaningful career.

In these cases, a step-by-step plan, breaking down larger goals into smaller and much more manageable steps, is really helpful

Which of your life goals (91) do you think would benefit from a step-by-step plan?

96 How I quit IT and found a better path

The genie thought experiment (91) set me on a quest for work that would be enjoyable, pay the bills *and* feel meaningful. But how? Friends' advice left me confused. Some were encouraging, but others said, 'Dream on!'

I needed a step-by-step plan:

1. Identify possible careers.

2. Research training and costs.

3. Work out the pros and cons of each option.

4. Decide on the right timescale.

And then … *drum roll* …

5. Embark on my new career.

It took over ten years to become a full-time therapist. It wouldn't have happened without a plan and a first step.

Make your own step-by-step plan for a cherished life goal. Take the first step.

97   Control the controllables like the Stoic Archer

Jenny is looking for her first job. After a month of rejection letters, she feels dejected. Then, like any good aspiring Stoic, Jenny decides to decipher what she can control.

> What can't I control? – *'The economic climate and whether my application gets accepted.'*
>
> What can I control? – *'My attitude and behaviour.'*

Jenny makes a plan:

- Commit to at least three job applications a day.
- Get a friend to look over my CV.
- Research what skills to learn to improve my chances.
- Remember the Stoic Archer (**12**)? Like a good archer, I need to focus on my preparation. If I miss the target, that's OK, too …

What goal can you start to get under control today?

98   Wrong destination!

It happens.

You are excited by the brochure's promise of sun and relaxation. Then you arrive to find a building site next to the hotel. And it rains all week.

But it's only one wasted week.

It's a bigger problem if your *life goals* don't make you happy.

What if *they* take you to the wrong destination?

99   Charlie – a cautionary tale

Charlie, a very nice chap, was very unhappy with his work. He was in a well-paid but stressful job. One sunny day, he saw his postman whistling happily as he did his job.

'I want to be like that!' thought Charlie.

So he became a postman.

Two years later, Charlie was in a badly paid job and even more stressed.

If you are going on a long journey, it's worth checking out whether the destination is all it's cracked up to be.

100   Are some life goals better than others?

Research says 'Yes'.

Goals related to finding fulfilling work, being in trusting close relationships, connecting with the world beyond oneself, and spirituality are all connected with higher levels of happiness.

Goals to do with financial success, physical attractiveness, and wanting to control or dominate people are associated with lower life satisfaction.

Perhaps you already knew this. Can't we all think of celebrities who are rich and attractive and have lots of power over others but who are completely miserable?

How about your own life goals? Are you barking up the wrong tree?

101 Uncontrollable externals

> 'Externals are not in my power; choice is. Where shall
> I seek good and evil? Within.'
>
> Epictetus, *Discourses* 2.5

Epictetus divides everything into two categories: those things that are up to us – our choices, voluntary actions and the way we think about things – *the internals* – and everything else, those things that are not up to us – *the externals*.

If you place value on externals, you become a hostage to fortune.

If you place value on internals, nothing can stop you being happy.

Where do you place value?

102 Is Emily placing too much value on externals?

Let's take another look at Emily's list of life goals (**92**):

1. Be a good mother, partner and daughter.

2. Have a successful career.

3. Leave the world a slightly better place.

4. Enjoy good friendships.

5. Develop my character so I become the best version of me.

Which of these life goals do you think will win Epictetus's approval?

Is she placing value on internals or externals?

103   Stoic life coaching, the Epictetus way

Suppose Emily could be transported back in time to get advice from Epictetus himself. This is what I imagine he would say (though be prepared for Epictetus's rather blunt style!) …

1. Be a good mother, partner and daughter. *A good goal – are you living up to it?*

2. Have a successful career. *Sounds like an external to me – how much control do you have over that?*

3. Leave the world a slightly better place. *Wretch! You have succeeded in aiming too high and too low. Too high because you can't control the outcome. Too low – why only make a slight difference?*

4. Enjoy good friendships. *If you mean 'having lots of friends', then that sounds like an external, not under your control. Focus on being a good friend, something over which you have complete control.*

5. Develop my character so I become the best version of me. *Maybe you are not a totally lost cause after all, Emily! But I can see we have plenty of work to do.*

How do you think Emily should revise her life goals in the light of Epictetus's comments?

104   Emily gets her life goals back under control

Helped by Epictetus's forthright feedback, Emily comes up with this revised list of life goals.

1. Be a good mother, partner and daughter.

2. ~~Have a successful career.~~ Do my best to ensure I have a successful career.

3. ~~Leave the world a slightly better place.~~ Do my best to leave the world a better place.

4. ~~Enjoy good friendships.~~ Be a good friend.

5. Develop my character so I become the best version of me.

Much better!

What do your own life goals look like when you focus only on the internals, under your control.

105   Leave La La Land

> 'No man is an island, entire of itself; every man /
> is a piece of the continent, a part of the main.'
>
> John Donne, *No Man Is an Island*

These words could just as easily have appeared in Marcus Aurelius's *Meditations*. Good life goals, according to Stoics, aim at internals not externals *and* emphasize our relationships.

Did you watch the 2016 film *La La Land*? The main characters, Mia and Sebastian, are both driven by career ambition – Mia to be a successful actress, Sebastian to own a jazz club. Both goals aim at externals.

(Major spoiler alert!)

They also choose ambition over relationships – leading to the not so happy ending in the film. Compare this with the fantastic Epilogue scene, where Mia and Sebastian prioritize differently.

The philosophies of *La La Land* and Stoicism are quite different.

Are any of your life goals too *La La Land*-ish?

106   Your key roles

Epictetus came up with a good safeguard against possible egocentricity and narcissism. It involves identifying your key roles.

Our roles are the glue which connect us to other people.

How do you define yours?

For each role below that applies to you, give yourself a rating out of 10 for importance (I) and achievement (A).

Role	Importance (I)	Achievement (A)
Mother/father		
Husband/wife/partner		
Daughter/son		
Friend		
Work		
Hobbies and interests		
Other (please specify)		

For example, if your role as a friend is moderately important, put I=6. If you are performing it pretty well, put A=7.

What do you notice?

107 Emily's key roles

Emily finds this way of thinking about her life intriguing. Here is her key role audit:

Role	Notes	Importance (I)	Achievement (A)
Mother	… of two lovely, but demanding, children! I wish I shouted at them less.	10	6
Wife	Although sometimes that feels like being a mother, too!	8	6
Daughter	Hmm, maybe I should give my parents a call.	6	7
Friend	I've probably neglected some friends – life is so busy these days.	5	6
Work	I'm a colleague, team member and manager. Oops – almost forgot our clients! I'm also an advisor to them. They aren't as important as my immediate family. I'm doing fine.	6	8
Hobbies and interests	I'm treasurer of the tennis club – though I'm not particularly suited to this task and haven't got time to play tennis.	3	2

Emily finds this exercise quite an eye-opener.

If you were her Stoic mentor, what tips might you offer?

108 The key roles audit

Two questions will help you get the most from your key roles audit:

1. Are you devoting enough energy to your most important roles?

2. Are you giving too much attention to less important roles?

Emily knows that her family is more important, yet she prioritizes work. She resolves to leave work on time and turn off her work phone when at home; and to read *Harry Potter* to her children at bedtime, which they have been begging her to do.

Emily realizes that she needs to resign as the tennis club treasurer, something she's been contemplating for a while.

What can you take from your audit?

109 A citizen of the world

> 'You are a citizen of the world ... act as the hand or foot
> would do, if they had reason and understood the
> constitution of nature.'

Epictetus, *Discourses* 2.10

Stoics think that we all have an additional *universal* role as a citizen of the world. In other words, we have a duty to play our part towards the common good.

What part? This will depend on the part you can play – your skills and your circumstances.

If you think of yourself as a citizen of the world, how would that affect your life goals and what you prioritize?

110　Schindler's list

German industrialist Oskar Schindler's heroism saving Jews from the death camps in World War II was made famous by Stephen Spielberg's Oscar-winning 1993 film, *Schindler's List*. Yet, prior to his heroic deeds, Schindler was not, by all accounts, a particularly principled man. A womanizer, gambler and opportunist, he initially hired Jewish workers in his factories simply because they were cheap labour.

Schindler found himself in a situation where he felt compassion for his Jewish workers and was able to help them. Fate put Schindler in a situation where he could do a lot of good. History judges him to be a hero.

Where can you do the most good?

111　Bah humbug!

I am sure you know the story of Charles Dickens' *A Christmas Carol* – retold in films like *Scrooged* and *The Muppet Christmas Carol*!

'Bah humbug!' exclaims the miser Ebenezer Scrooge when asked to join in with the spirit of Christmas goodwill. But that's before he gets visits from the Three Ghosts of Christmas.

The Ghost of Christmas Past reminds Scrooge that he wasn't always so curmudgeonly.

The Ghost of Christmas Present contrasts Scrooge's own lonely existence with the joy in the Cratchit household.

But the Ghost of Christmas Future provides Scrooge with the biggest wake-up call. Scrooge is shown his own funeral. What a sad occasion it looks, not a single soul mourning his passing. All there is to show for his time on Earth is a neglected grave. Scrooge understands that unless he changes, this is to be his destiny. He is shaken into becoming much kinder, resulting in him also becoming a lot happier.

Dickens thought that there was a lesson here for his readers: we all have the potential for kindness and generosity *and* for pettiness and greed. We will be happier if we choose the former.

Is Dickens right?

112 The Stoic Three Ghosts exercise – Part I: A message from the past

Jessie, in her mid-twenties, is quite stressed by work. Her friends keep telling her to 'chill out!'. Although she is no Scrooge, Jessie is fascinated by these new perspectives offered by the Stoic Three Ghosts.

First, she considers the question posed by the Stoic ghost from the past …

'Think of a time when you were leading a better life. What qualities helped you be happier?'

Jessie jots down the following:

'I was happier when I was at university. What helped? Well, I made an effort to spend time with friends – and I enjoyed learning.'

It's not difficult for Jessie to decipher the message – to be more sociable and get back to learning.

What message would you get from the Stoic ghost from your past?

113 The Stoic Three Ghosts exercise – Part II: A message from the present

Think of people who are happier and leading a better life than you right now. What qualities are they exhibiting that you don't?

Jessie picks her friend Sue, who seems genuinely happy. 'She never gets wound up by anything and always finds time to enjoy life.'

She can use Stoicism to be more Sue-like and become happier.

Who would you want to emulate?

114   The Stoic Three Ghosts exercise – Part III: A message from the future

What might your future look like if you do not make positive change? What's the worst-case scenario?

Jessie doesn't like this question at all! Yet she wonders if, as in *A Christmas Carol*, it will have the most impact.

Jessie closes her eyes and imagines working long hours, losing contact with her friends and getting married only to her job. Not so different from Scrooge after all!

She realizes the urgency of finding a better work–life balance. First step – a spa break with friends. After that – well, time to think about changing jobs.

What unpleasant fate might the ghost from the future warn you about? What can you do to avert it?

115   The route to inner peace

From Paul Wilson – mental health and well-being professional and student of Stoicism

We are bombarded with negative news. It would be so easy to despair of humanity and to lead selfish, careless, brutish lives. When I feel that way, I turn to Marcus Aurelius. He reminds me that each day I have work to do – as a human being. I find peace and purpose in that advice – power, too.

That simple sentiment reminds me of my daily choice: to be a positive or a negative force in the lives of others. So, I set about that work to the best of my ability. I try to add to the store of micro-kindnesses that occur quietly each day. I measure my worth in unfashionable metrics, like smiles, thanks and reciprocal courtesies. I know of no purer and more sustainable source of self-esteem than good conduct. The Stoics called it *arete* (the Greek word for excellence or virtue). It offers the most direct route to inner peace, and anyone can practise it. We can each sculpt our own statue, one good deed at a time.

116   Your own life coaching session with Epictetus

Life goals should …

- be internal, not external – so that they are under your control
- help you fulfil your key roles in life
- contribute to the common good.

Imagine that you have a life coaching session with Epictetus booked for tomorrow. He wants to see your top 5 life goals. What would they be?

1.

2.

3.

4.

5.

117   Emily reviews her life goals

Despite his forthright feedback – or perhaps because of it – Emily found her Epictetus-style coaching session (103) very illuminating. Having learned more, she drafts a final version for Epictetus to evaluate.

1. Be a good mother, partner and daughter.

2. ~~Have a successful career.~~ Do my best to ensure I have a successful career (as this much is under my control). Be a good manager, colleague and advisor (and so fulfil my key roles).

3. ~~Leave the world a slightly better place.~~ Do my best to leave the world a better place by looking for opportunities to do so.

4. ~~Friendships.~~ Be a good friend.

5. ~~Develop my character so I become the best version of me.~~ Work especially on my self-control regarding work–life balance.

How do you imagine Epictetus might react?

118   Another coaching session with Epictetus!

Epictetus loves Emily's new life goals! But never one to let you rest on your laurels, Epictetus adds: 'That's excellent, Emily. Now I want you to think what could stop you achieving them.'

Life might get in the way.

Jot down three things that could help Emily – and you – to remember to implement your goals.

119   Top tips for working towards your life goals

Here's what my clients have found most helpful during Stoic life coaching sessions:

- Use the morning premeditation to rehearse how to work towards your goal today. Consider likely obstacles and how to overcome them.
- Think of difficult emotions that might get in the way (such as fear of failure) and how to manage them.
- The virtues lens – which virtues can help you achieve your goals? (See **36**.)
- Print out your list of life goals and put them somewhere you can see them.
- Keep your step-by-step plan up to date.
- Share your goals with encouraging people.
- In the evening, do a Stoic review focusing on your life goals.
- Write a letter (or email) to yourself written from the perspective of your Stoic life coach, to be opened in the future.

120 A letter to Emily from her Stoic life coach

To be opened one year from now.

Dear Future Emily,

For pity's sake, don't live as if you're immortal!
Your children will be a year older by the time you read this – fate permitting! Soon enough you will be the one begging to read to them at bedtime. Have you got through Harry Potter and the Goblet of Fire yet? I do hope you all enjoyed it. But remember, your key motivation was to be a good parent.

How about your work–life balance?

Have you resigned as tennis club treasurer yet?

Are you finding time to be a good friend?

Last time we spoke, you said you were about 60 per cent Stoic.

You wanted to be closer to 70 by now. How would you rate yourself?

What's your next step?

You can do it!

Your Stoic Life Coach

Emily's answers would have pleased her Stoic life coach – well, perhaps not if he were Epictetus!

Follow-up

- Compare your answers to **91** and **116** to see how much more Stoic you have become.
- The essential entry in this chapter is **116**: Your own life coaching session with Epictetus.
- Keep working on the tips in **119**. Consider using a step-by-step plan to help.

CHAPTER 5
SELF-CONTROL

Self-control is the ability to do the right thing, even when you're tempted to do otherwise. Experts widely agree that self-control is crucial for lasting happiness and success. Yet, many people struggle with it. When researchers ask people about their strengths, self-control comes bottom.

Stoicism can help, though!

Self-control is partly about willpower and strengthening its 'muscle'. But it's also about understanding *why* it's so important and learning how to exercise self-control, without relying too much on willpower.

We'll be combining ancient Stoic wisdom with modern research illustrated by real-life examples. You'll hear how Kasey, the editor of this book, used Stoic principles to lose 115 pounds. A client of mine – I'll call him Roy – applied them to stop a cocaine habit in its tracks. I too, dear reader, face self-control challenges and will share how I got on employing these methods while writing this chapter.

The ideas contained here can be applied to many other types of self-control challenges, such as social media overuse and other vices. It's not intended as a substitute for medical treatment, though, so please seek professional advice if appropriate.

121   Self-control check-in

How would you rate your self-control most of the time? Score yourself on the following statements, using 4 = That's me; 3 = Partially true; 2 = Neutral; 1 = Mainly untrue; and 0 = Not me at all.

1. I find it difficult to resist temptation.

2. I eat unhealthily.

3. I drink too much alcohol.

4. I don't exercise as much as I should.

[ ]

5. I have other bad habits I desire to change.

[ ]

6. I'm not good at exercising self-control.

[ ]

Now add up your points. Your score will run from 0 (most self-control) to 24 (lowest self-control). Don't worry if you score highly: many people do before they learn how to improve. Take the test now, and then again once you've finished the chapter.

122 The marshmallow test

Imagine you are four years old and faced with this dilemma.

In front of you is a tasty marshmallow, which you're free to eat right now. But if you wait a few minutes, you'll be rewarded with a second marshmallow. Would you have eaten the marshmallow or waited? Psychologist Walter Mischel famously reported that passing this 'marshmallow test' predicted academic success years later, better than IQ tests. Research suggests many other benefits of self-control in terms of wealth, health, relationships and happiness.

How could self-control help you?

123 Your inner Homer Simpson

'The most powerful people have power
over themselves.'

Seneca, *Letters* 110.34

Who do you want in the driving seat?

Your inner Homer Simpson who can't see past the next doughnut?

Or a more Stoic version of yourself who takes long-term consequences into account?

Where in your life would you like to take control back from your inner Homer?

124 What's your personal self-control challenge?

The three real-life stories you'll be hearing about in this chapter relate to weight, drugs and health. There are many other areas where self-control can help, such as:

- drink
- sex
- social media use
- quickness to anger
- boasting
- lack of exercise.

To get the most out of this chapter, please take a few moments to pick a specific self-control challenge to rise to this month.

125 Why bother?

Why exactly should you bother to change?

If you scored very low on the self-test in 121 (under 10), then perhaps you don't need to bother.

Otherwise, perhaps Epictetus's forthright reminder might provide an answer:

> 'How long, then, will you put off thinking yourself
> worthy of the highest improvements and follow
> the distinctions of reason?'
>
> *Handbook 51*

126   What shall I change?

Maybe you still need reassurance that you're focusing on the right area to change.

A simple, useful approach is to write down the pros and cons of change.

Take a piece of paper (or use your electronic device) and write down three headings – Pros, Cons and Conclusion.

What does reason tell you to do?

127   Time for a social media diet?

Cassie is thinking about whether her self-control challenge should be to reduce her excessive social media use. She uses the Pros, Cons and Conclusion method.

Question

Should I keep using social media like I do?

Pros

'I can keep up with my family and friends.'

'It's good for my online business.'

'I can find support in tough times.'

Cons

'I feel addicted, a scrolling zombie.'

'It's very stimulating, so it keeps me up at night.'

'I feel inadequate, even though I know these posts are just people's "highlight reels".'

'I base my self-worth on how many likes I get.'

'I feel isolated when I'm sitting at home and see pictures of people socializing.'

'I'm often triggered by political rants that oppose my views and it sets the tone for the day. I've lost some meaningful friendships over this crap.'

Conclusion

'Seeing it in black and white, it's so obvious! Social media is toxic for me, and I'm going to cut down!'

It's not just Cassie, either. A 2018 British study tied social media use to poor sleep, which is associated with depression, memory loss and poor academic performance.

Is reducing your social media use the challenge for you?

128   'But it's OK in moderation, right?'

'Roy', a successful young professional, worked hard in the week and played hard at weekends. He and his friends liked to party, and that often meant plenty of drinks followed by a few lines of coke.

Roy was quite certain that he wasn't addicted to cocaine and was wondering whether what he described as very moderate use was

OK. Not wanting to prejudge the issue, I asked Roy to research this objectively.

He found the results pretty shocking. Among the short-term dangers of even moderate cocaine use were increased risk of anxiety, sleep problems and heart attack. Longer-term vulnerabilities included severe cognitive impairment and permanent cardiovascular damage – not to mention the substantial risk of addiction. When cocaine is mixed with alcohol, as in his case, the risk of sudden heart problems became significantly higher.

This research profoundly affected Roy. Would it be worth it to research the possible ill effects of your own challenging behaviour?

129   Pleasure or true happiness?

There's one extremely good Stoic reason for self-control that is often missed.

What's that?

Ask yourself this question: Do tempting things – junk food, illicit sex, drink, drugs and the rest – actually bring lasting happiness? Or temporary pleasure?

Killjoy!

Stoics are not killjoys at all. Genuine joy – the satisfying feeling from good human relationships and from behaving well – is prized by the Stoic.

But isn't pleasure good?

It depends on the use that you make of it. Pleasures are not *bad* or *good*, but healthy or unhealthy. For example, Epictetus says that all tragedy comes from attaching too much value to external things, including those that bring pleasure.

Temporary pleasure at a high cost? Or a life well lived bringing lasting happiness?

What's your call?

130   Don't put fuel on the fire

Faced with this stark choice, many people would choose true happiness over fleeting pleasure but wonder if it's OK to enjoy pleasure in moderation. Can't we have our cake and eat it?

The Stoic answer is that it all depends. If you genuinely can enjoy pleasures without becoming addicted to them, then yes. But the problem is that, by its nature, pleasure is addictive. As Epictetus wrote:

> Every habit and every faculty is confirmed and
> strengthened by the corresponding acts … if you do not
> wish to acquire the habit, abstain from doing it, and acquire
> the habit of doing something else instead … know that
> you have not merely done ill, but that you have strengthened
> the habit, and, as it were, put fuel on the fire. … you must take
> account not only of this one defeat, but of the fact that
> you have fed your lack of self-control and strengthened it.
>
> *Discourses* 2.18

Today, ask yourself whether any of your bad habits could be the start of a slippery slope.

131   A slippery slope

Roy learned that, far from being harmless, there was a clear pathway from occasional cocaine use to addiction.

When you take cocaine, more dopamine is produced in the brain and you feel good. Your brain now craves this rush of good feeling, and so you take more. It then begins to lose its ability to feel good from healthy sources of dopamine and becomes reliant on cocaine ... to feel even close to good. So, you take more ...

The Stoics thought that any pleasure could be the start of a similar slippery slope.

Have you become dependent on what you once saw as an innocent indulgence?

132   Who do you want to be?

From a Stoic perspective, your decision about whether to be self-controlled is an existential choice.

In his characteristically direct way, Epictetus puts it like this:

> You must watch, you must labour, you must get the better
> of certain appetites ... if you have a mind to purchase serenity,
> freedom, and tranquillity ... You must be either good or bad. You
> must cultivate either your own reason or else externals, apply
> yourself either to things within or without you; that is,
> be either a philosopher, or one of the mob.
>
> *Handbook 29*

Who do you want to be?

133   A duty to yourself

Kasey, this book's editor, struggled with weight issues when she was younger. She was well aware of the usual arguments for losing weight. But one of the Stoic arguments we have just heard had a more profound impact. Losing weight was a *duty* to herself. She writes:

'While it's wonderful to feel confident in your appearance, looks fade. Virtue isn't derived from your appearance. It's born out of why we did the things we did: because they were the right things to do. This is something you must do, if nothing prevents you, for yourself and others that need you in good health.

'Besides, no one is going to do it for you. You're going to do it or it won't happen. It's as simple as that.'

> 'First say to yourself, who you wish to be: then do accordingly.'
>
> Epictetus, *Discourses* 3.23

134   I want to change – but how?

So, you've decided you'd like to change. The next question is – how?

Kasey initially found her challenge overwhelming:

'When I set out to lose weight, I knew I needed to lose at least 100 pounds. However, as hell-bent as I was, once I put "1–0–0" on my whiteboard, those three digits stared me down like a trio of hoodlums I owed money to. I felt surrounded and the road ahead seemed to grow longer and longer. All I could think was that 100 pounds is the combined average weight of two seven-year-olds. I was about to attempt to lose two full-grown kids! Not even toddlers!'

What advice would you have given Kasey?

135   Make it easier

Kasey felt overwhelmed when she thought of losing 100 pounds. But that wasn't the only way to look at it. Once again, Epictetus provided good advice.

> 'You ought to practise in small things and go on from them to greater.'
>
> Epictetus, *Discourses* 1.18

Kasey realized that how she framed her challenge made a big difference to her motivation:

'I could just as easily phrase the goal as *I need to lose 10 pounds ten times*. Personally, I erased two of the three numerals from the whiteboard and replaced them with the number nine. For some reason, I found that the 90-pound goal wasn't nearly as intimidating as 100 pounds. I mean, once I got there, what was another ten? I decided this time, the goal, the numbers, weren't going to have any power over my mental state.'

Could breaking down your self-control challenge into easier steps help you?

136   Know thyself

One of the Delphic maxims inscribed in the forecourt of the Temple of Apollo was 'Know thyself'. Socrates and countless other ancient philosophers agreed.

Zeno, the founder of Stoicism, stated: 'Nothing is more hostile to a firm grasp on knowledge than self-deception.'

When it comes to willpower, we might all have less of it than we think. Modern research suggests that willpower is a limited resource, which ebbs and flows.

But this is not necessarily a cause for despair. If you can't rely on willpower, why not use your *wisdom* to exercise self-control instead?

Imagine that James wants to stop eating chocolate but finds that difficult. He could try …

■ capitalizing on times when his willpower is high. *James shops after he's eaten, when he feels too full to want chocolate.*

■ reward substitution – replacing the thing you want to avoid with something else. *James buys dark chocolate instead.*

- the 20-second rule – making the good habit 20 seconds easier than the bad one. *James puts his stash of chocolate somewhere hard to access.*
- a self-control contract – *James makes a pledge to a cause he dislikes if he eats milk chocolate.*

A Stoic sage wouldn't need such 'self-control hacks'. But they might be useful for those of us who are still making progress. Which of these tips could help you?

137   Self-control is a social process

You don't have to go it alone. An accountability partner can help coach you to keep your commitment.

The Stoics understood that self-control is a *social* process. Epictetus warned specifically against keeping the wrong kind of company:

> Be assured that if a person be ever so sound themself, yet,
> if their companion be infected, they who converse with them
> will be infected likewise.

Handbook 33

Elsewhere, he memorably told us that:

> It's impossible to rub up against someone who is covered with soot
> and not get sooty oneself.

Discourses 3.16.3

Who, in your life, would make a good *soot-free* accountability partner?

138   What's keeping the problem going?

It's helpful to understand what keeps a problem going. It's another example of what the Stoics called *wisdom*!

Kasey found answering this idea to be immensely valuable in her successful quest to lose over 100 pounds:

'It was my cravings for junk food and my giving in to them that led me to be overweight. Sure, I could have just said, "OK, I'm just not going to eat junk food." Without understanding why I craved these things and why it was so harmful, however, I would have just resumed my old diet eventually. This time, though, I researched the science behind my cravings. When I ate simple carbohydrates, my pancreas dumped insulin into my bloodstream and raised my blood sugar … *really fast*. This felt great in the moment. Yet as those moments became more and more fleeting, I went back to satisfy that craving repeatedly. This led me to being obese.

'So, like any high, I decided to view it as a cheap thrill. I would remind myself that if I could ride out the craving for the high, slowly but surely I would train my body and mind to stop looking for it. Returning to weight loss without understanding the *why*, another bag of crisps would have just been another bag of crisps – not the temporary high that may lead to long-term damage.'

What's keeping your problem going?

139   Your personal Olympics

'Remember that the hour of struggle is come,
the Olympic contest is here and you may put off
no longer, and that one day and one action determines
whether the progress you have achieved is lost or maintained.

'This was how Socrates attained perfection, paying heed to nothing but reason, in all that he encountered. And if you are not yet Socrates yet ought you to live as one who would wish to be a Socrates.'

Epictetus, *Handbook* 51

Roy is about to face *his* personal Olympics. He's decided cocaine in moderation isn't an option, so he will abstain completely.

Then, after a long hard week, a little voice suggests otherwise …

'Come on, mate,' pleads the voice of temptation. 'You've earned it. Don't be a killjoy! A little won't hurt.'

Can you help Roy to 'be a Socrates'?

How would you respond to the voice of temptation?

140   Your inner Socrates

Roy prepared himself in advance by developing the following rational responses:

Temptation: Come on, mate, you've earned it.

Response: *Earned what? I'll feel terrible tomorrow.*

Temptation: Don't be a killjoy!

Response: *I'm not being a killjoy. I'm building resilience.*

Temptation: A little won't do any harm …

Response: *The research proves otherwise. It is likely to do harm in both the short and long term. Always bear this in mind, too. Casual use is the slippery slope to addiction.*

Forewarned is forearmed. How can your own inner Socrates help you pre-emptively respond to temptation?

141   Delay acting on impulse

Nobel Prize-winning academic Daniel Kahneman popularized the idea that we have two ways of thinking – fast and slow. We have a fast, automatic gear, which allows us to decide quickly. We also have a slow, manual gear, which enables us to assess situations logically.

While the Stoics did not use the same terminology, they recognized this distinction. When it comes to self-control, they knew to pause to allow time for slow, cool, manual thinking.

As Epictetus said:

> 'Try, therefore, in the first place, not to be hurried away with the appearance. For if you once gain time and respite, you will more easily command yourself.'
>
> *Handbook* 20

How do you think you could best delay acting on impulse?

Remember the four-year-olds who resisted eating the marshmallow (122)? Here are some of their successful tactics:

- closing their eyes so they couldn't see the marshmallow
- remembering they could have two if they waited
- singing to themselves.

How best can you resist acting on impulse?

142   Get some detachment

Acceptance and commitment therapy (ACT), which combines elements of CBT and mindfulness, suggests an alternative to directly challenging the voice of temptation (140).

The idea is to take the wind out of its sails by seeing it for what it is – just the voice of temptation – rather than what it claims to be – good advice. We've already seen this in action in this chapter: **123:** Your inner Homer Simpson and **128:** 'But it's OK in moderation, right?'.

What could you say to yourself to create detachment when you're tempted?

143   Don't get carried away

'When I see a beautiful woman, I do not say to myself,
"I wish she were mine!" and "How lucky her husband is!"
For he who says that will say, "How lucky is an adulterer!"
Nor do I picture the next scene: the woman present
and stripping and lying down by my side.'

Epictetus, *Discourses* 2.18

Just as Netflix plays previews to entice you, so *temptation* will give you a preview of all the delights it offers, given the chance. Epictetus reminds us that we don't have to watch. Much better to play a preview of how we'll feel tomorrow depending on our choice …

'When you imagine some pleasure, beware that it does
not carry you away, like other imaginations. Wait a while,
and give yourself pause. Next remember two things:
how long you will enjoy the pleasure, and also how long
you will afterwards repent and reproach yourself.
And set on the other side the joy and self-satisfaction
you will feel if you refrain.'

Epictetus, *Handbook* 34

Epictetus's words can be adapted to any self-control challenge.

Think about how it will feel when you take your power back from the chokehold of temptations that don't serve you.

144 Rejoice!

'Count the days when you were not angry. I used to be angry every
day, then every other day, then every three days, then every four.
But if you miss thirty days, then sacrifice to God: for the
habit is first weakened and then wholly destroyed.'

Epictetus, *Discourses* 1.18

Epictetus recommends keeping track of all the consecutive days you've
succeeded in your self-control challenge. That's good advice and it's
even better to rejoice *every* time you succeed, thereby providing a
reward and positive reinforcement for self-control.

When you congratulate yourself in this way, you experience the good
Stoic emotion of joy – pride in doing the right thing.

Enjoy your self-control journey and take pride in every successful step.

145 A CURE for a lack of self-control

You can CURE the problem of self-control in these four stages:

C – Challenge yourself to master self-control in a specific area.

U – Understand why it matters, what keeps the problem going, and
ask yourself what's likely to work for you.

R – Resist temptation – employ your inner Socrates by developing
rational responses and time for logic to get into the driving seat.

E – Enjoy your sense of achievement every time you exercise self-
control.

146 My personal self-control challenge

Having reached an age where I need to be more health conscious, my
doctor advised me to monitor my blood pressure. It averaged 140/91 – on
the high side. We scheduled a Christmas Eve consultation to discuss options.

A lot of my friends are taking medication for hypertension and I expected this outcome. It turned out that the doctor wasn't going to make things so easy for me …

'Well, Mr LeBon …' he started, 'you have high blood pressure and it should come down to reduce the risk of serious problems. But it's not in the range where medication, which can have side-effects, is essential. I recommend some lifestyle changes first. How do you feel about that?'

'Apprehensive' would have been my honest answer. I've never followed a successful diet in my life!

'I recommend the DASH diet,' he continued. 'Would you be willing to try that? We'll schedule a follow-up.'

Fate had handed me my own self-control challenge …

147   A DASH of Stoicism

It was one thing for the doctor to tell me to follow the DASH diet – quite another to follow it. It would mean eating more fruit, vegetables, fibre and exercising, and cutting down on red meat, alcohol, salt and sweets. Having a sweet tooth, I anticipated this would be challenging.

As recommended in **126**, I drew up this balance sheet:

Pros

1. I want to be healthy – for myself and others.

2. I want to avoid side-effects of medications.

3. The DASH diet will help me lose weight and lower blood pressure.

4. I like the food options in this diet.

It was hard to resist this conclusion:

'I should try the DASH diet. I've never applied Stoicism to helping me stick to a diet – now is my chance!'

Remembering the fridge full of Christmas goodies, I committed to a start date – 1 January.

148   Understanding my problem

January 2022 arrived, and after a Christmas period spent eating and drinking too much and exercising too little, my blood pressure had changed from 140/90 to … 145/95.

Well, at least that proved a connection between diet and blood pressure!

It was time to understand the situation better. My own cycle was hunger – sugar – temporary relief – crash – more hunger – more sugar – rather like that described by Kasey. I also realized that I wasn't drinking enough water, and dehydration played a part in my cravings.

Knowing myself, I wasn't sure I had enough willpower to resist temptation if there was any chocolate in the house. So, I avoided the confectionery aisle. I realized that I liked a lot of the healthy stuff – some fruit, some vegetables, brown rice instead of white rice … To cut down on salt, I absolutely had to cut down on processed food.

I recruited a friend as an accountability partner.

I was ready for action!

149   Tim's progress – day 14

I took my blood pressure every day and followed the DASH diet. I was drinking more water and my appetite reduced. I bought chocolate substitutes, but although they had fewer calories, they increased hunger. So, I would need to cut them out. I started to make my own meals rather than eating processed food and developed a taste for fish. I mustered up enough willpower to refuse alcohol when offered.

I began to see progress. After a week, my blood pressure had reduced to 135/87 – getting closer to my target of 119/79.

Still, I faced challenges. My friends wanted to have a curry night, and it didn't seem fair to suggest going to a salad bar instead …

What does a good Stoic do in these situations? Time for some moderation and wisdom!

I researched 'Indian food calories' and learned that while creamy curries should be avoided, tandoori grills were full of protein.

Self-control doesn't mean abstinence.

150   Tim's progress – day 33

Today my blood pressure is 119/79. I have achieved my target. How did I do it?

By understanding the problem, my own limitations and how to overcome obstacles.

I fear that Epictetus would not be celebrating my success … yet. I hear his words ringing in my ears:

'Wretch, you still value externals too much! You wouldn't need to keep chocolate out of the house if you'd really got my Stoic message.'

'But, Epictetus, didn't you also say that we need to know our limitations?'

'Yes, that's why I am reminding you of yours!'

Ouch!

Follow-up

■ Retake the test in **121**.

■ The essential entry in this chapter is **145**: A CURE for a lack of self-control.

■ What's your next self-control challenge?

CHAPTER 6
COURAGE

Courage means doing the right thing even in situations where you may feel fear or risk personal cost.

If you want to be the best version of yourself, could courage help? Did you know there is a Stoic shortcut to courage? You will once you've read this chapter!

Sometimes, though, more is needed to increase your willingness to act or reduce fear. We will be drawing on real examples of people being inspired by Stoicism to be courageous, supplementing these with tips from both the ancient Stoics and modern psychologists.

For Stoics, moral courage – standing up for what is right – has always been the main focus when discussing courage. Important as this is, it's valuable to see courage more broadly – to include such qualities as bravery, grit, persistence and determination. This chapter can help you build these, too.

As always, it's going to be helpful if you can set yourself a personal challenge when reading this chapter. What would you like to achieve by the end of this chapter that requires you to be courageous?

151　What is courage?

Courage isn't to be confused with recklessness or bravado.

As Seneca reminds us:

> 'Courage is not thoughtless rashness, or love of danger,
> or the courting of fear-inspiring objects; it is the
> knowledge which enables us to distinguish between
> that which is evil and that which is not.'

Letters 85

It would be thoughtless rashness, not true courage, to jump in to try to save a drowning child when you can't swim yourself.

It would be immoral, not true courage, to rob a bank, even if you had to overcome fear.

Courage requires both knowing what is right and having the will to do it, even when that's challenging.

152   Courage - self-check-in

On a scale of 0 (not at all) to 10 (totally), how much are the following statements true in general for you?

1. I do what I think is right even at the risk of some personal cost.

2. I complete things that matter even when I don't feel motivated.

3. I strive to act courageously whenever opportunities arrive.

4. I don't let anxiety get in the way of me doing worthwhile things.

The higher your overall score (0–40), the more courageous you are. What is your total?

Do any of your answers suggest a specific area for development?

153   Susan Fowler, Stoic whistleblower

'When you do a thing because you have determined
that it ought to be done, never avoid being seen doing it,
even if the opinion of the multitude is going to condemn you.
For if your action is wrong, then avoid doing it altogether,
but if it is right, why do you fear those who
will rebuke you wrongly?'

Epictetus, *Handbook* 35

In her memoir *Whistleblower: My Unlikely Journey to Silicon Valley and Speaking Out against Injustice*, Susan Fowler describes how reading and rereading Epictetus – especially the above passage – encouraged her to whistleblow her concerns about sexism and harassment at Uber.

Fowler wrote a blog post in 2017 describing the culture at Uber, including her personal experience of sexual harassment which had gone unpunished even after she'd reported it. The post made quite a stir. A proper investigation took place and CEO Travis Kalanick resigned. Stoicism had kick-started Silicon Valley's own #MeToo moment.

Fowler understood that Stoicism meant speaking out for what was right. Though she lost her job, she gained much more – her self-worth.

154   Tackling Stoicism

From Trevor Munro-Clark – CBT/EMDR psychotherapist

As a psychological therapist, I generally work from the reasonable distance of a comfortable chair. However, I was once required to act quickly and decisively, which involved rugby-tackling my patient to the floor to maintain their physical safety – even though I wasn't entirely convinced it was the right thing to do, and it had the strong potential of demolishing our therapeutic relationship. To physically tackle your clients is generally not discussed in psychotherapist training!

Although I am a New Zealander, I felt little confidence in my schoolboy tackling techniques. Nevertheless, I believe channelling my Stoic virtue of courage and 'doing the right thing' provided me with the inner strength to commit to the right action.

Stoic courage isn't just about facing fear, although I was fearful of what might happen to my client if I hadn't intervened (and the potential threat to my career if I had got it wrong). I saw my fear of failure as less relevant than the duty of care to protect the vulnerable, sometimes even from themselves.

155   The best response is to dive in

From Alison McCone – follower of Modern Stoicism

I boarded the school bus for the journey to new school number five. Alone in the front seat, I felt the glare of 15 country bumpkins as they whispered and giggled at the back. Mortification does not even come close to describing how I felt. Being a Brit blowing into Eire following a three-year stopover in Gibraltar didn't help. But I did help myself. I reached out to others and made friends.

Anyway, we teens were all fish out of water in one way or another, with much more in common than individual differences. Many years later, as my fondness for Stoicism grew, I learned that feeling like a fish out of water is just that – a feeling. *The best response is to dive in*. This is my Stoic approach to living. Fortitude to brave the journey on the bus known as 'The Spud', wisdom to know the value of every person I meet, temperance to monitor my emotional turbulence, and justice for others who need understanding.

156   The Stoic shortcut to courage

The Stoic shortcut to courage is simple, according to Marcus Aurelius:

'To stop discussing what a good person should be and to be that person.'

Meditations 10.16

Don't overthink.

Just do the right thing, now.

157   The courage quotient

The Stoic shortcut – do the right thing, now – is a superb starting point. I recommend it as one of your personal mantras.

Sometimes, though, we need more. We can increase courage by increasing our willingness to act and by reducing our fear. Psychologist Robert Biswas-Diener proposes the following equation:

Courage equals *willingness to act* divided by *fear*.

He calls this 'the courage quotient'.

Susan (**153**) increased her willingness to act by rereading Epictetus.

Trevor (**154**) instinctively knew that his duty of concern overrode any concerns about his career.

Alison (**155**) reduced her fear by understanding that others were like her.

Think of a situation where you need courage. What reminders would help you?

158   Stand up for your beliefs

'The only thing necessary for the triumph of evil is that good people do nothing.'

Attributed to Edmund Burke

Courage begins with a choice: the decision to stand up for something you believe in rather than keep quiet or avoid the issue.

What are the possible costs of your inaction?

159   Remember the difference courage will make

Lisa, a nurse, worries that a colleague is not fit to practise. Patients' lives are at stake. Lisa wonders whether she should report her colleague.

A little voice inside her raises a doubt: 'My colleague will discover it's me who reported her. That will be awkward.'

Then a louder voice, the voice of courage, reminds her of how she would feel if she did nothing and a patient died.

'Potentially saving a life counts more than embarrassment,' says this louder voice of courage.

Lisa reports her concern. She wakes up the next day certain that she has done the right thing.

What is the voice of courage telling you?

160   Pick a role model for courage

'We need to set our affections on one good person and keep them constantly before our eyes, so that we may live as if they were watching us and do everything as if they saw what we were doing.'

Epicurus, quoted in Seneca

A key Stoic technique is to aim to emulate role models. Who would you choose as a role model for courage? It could be one of the Stoics, a historical figure (like Rosa Parks or Gandhi) or someone you've personally known. Imagine what your role model would do in your situation.

Seneca suggests an interesting twist when he approvingly quotes Epicurus's recommendation that we imagine our role model watching us at all times.

List what makes your role model courageous. Meditate on these things and strive to embody some of these admirable traits today.

161   The courage of Socrates

Socrates was probably the historical figure most admired by the Stoics.

Famously, when awaiting execution, he refused his friends' offers to help him escape. One reason for Socrates' courageous behaviour was his belief that it would be unjust for him to disobey the law. He wanted to do the right thing, even though it led to his death.

Another reason is quoted at the end of Epictetus's *Handbook*:

> 'Anytus and Meletus have power to put me to death,
> but not to harm me.'

Plato, *Apology* 30c

Socrates clearly took the idea that doing the right thing mattered much more than anything else very seriously! He was also famous for asking everyone he met awkward questions (the chief reason he was put to death).

If Socrates was watching you today, what might he be asking you?

162   Cato and the oracle before battle

Cato the Younger is the Stoic most revered for his courage.

Before a big battle with Julius Caesar, everybody kept telling Cato to seek advice from the oracle to find out his chances of success. Cato would have none of it.

'Why bother to ask the oracle?' he replied (in so many words). 'If the shrine tells me we're going to win, I'm going to fight Caesar. If the shrine tells me we're going to lose, I'm still going to fight Caesar, because it's the right thing to do – we're opposing a dictatorship.'

Or, as US movie actor John Wayne used to say, 'A man's gotta do what a man's gotta do.'

163   The courage family

When a leading group of psychologists decided to put together a classification of virtues and character strengths (the Values in Action Inventory, or VIA), they included courage as one of their six key virtues.

They helpfully broke courage down into four qualities: bravery, perseverance, honesty and zest. There are other, similar qualities in what might be called the 'courage family'.

What might we call courage when we don't give up on a hard task? *Persistence, zest and grit.*

What are the qualities we need to speak up for ourselves and what we believe in? *Assertiveness, confidence and belief.*

How about when we tell an awkward truth – such as telling someone they're smelly? *Honesty, integrity and truthfulness.*

What do we call it when we overcome our nerves, for example if we are asked to do a public speech? *Bravery, guts and determination.*

Which of the qualities in the courage family are going to be most helpful to you if you want to be the best version of yourself?

164 Good things aren't always served up to us on a plate

Sometimes life runs smoothly – your work, love life and friendships and family are all going swimmingly. But very often, they do not – and that's when courage can turn things around.

Obstacles can come in all kinds of shapes and sizes including difficult people, financial challenges, poor weather, illness and our own negative thinking.

- Have all your relationships and friendships always run smoothly, or do you sometimes have to work hard to maintain them?

- How about your career? Could you do with help overcoming obstacles to you having a more fulfilling job?

- Did you ever have to work hard over years to develop a particular skill – like a sport or playing a musical instrument? How about when it came to completing a big project like renovating a house?

- Where could you benefit most from courage in your life right now?

165 Set yourself a courage challenge

It's good to set yourself a personal challenge so you can use the ideas in this chapter to help you be more courageous. What's yours going to be?

Perhaps you want to be like Trevor (154) and take any opportunities that come your way to put your best foot forward?

Perhaps, like Alison (155), there's a particular challenge you need to dive into?

Or, maybe, you would like to work gradually towards a goal which requires courage?

Can the previous exercise (164) help you decide on a specific challenge?

You might like to review your core values (Chapter 4) and think about which of your core values requires courage so you can live up to them.

Spend a few moments deciding on a personal courage challenge. Jot it down so you can review how you got on at the end of this chapter.

166 We can all be courageous

People write themselves off too easily.

'I could never be as brave as Susan Fowler let alone Cato, Socrates or John Wayne!' confides Jane.

'I'm just not a good enough person,' suggests Robbie.

The Stoics would not agree. They believe that we all have the capacity for virtue, even if we don't know it. Chances are that you have shown courage many times in your life, even if that hasn't been acknowledged by anyone, not even yourself.

Spend a few moments running through this checklist to help you discover that you're more courageous than you may think.

- When have you done the right thing, even when there was some risk to yourself?
- When has your persistence been rewarded with success, despite setbacks?
- When have you achieved when others doubted you?

167 Recall past successes

'Think of good things that you've done; reflect on when you've shown good character.'

Seneca, *Letters* 78.18

Jane found doing the checklist helpful … She realizes that she has been brave on many occasions: 'I gave birth, so I know I can endure pain.'

Robbie also sees that he was underestimating himself: 'I spent a few hours listening to my friend when he was stressed out.'

Jot down some examples of your courage.

Bring them to mind the next time you need to give yourself a positive pep talk.

168 The power of 'not yet'

'If a thing is humanly possible and appropriate, consider it also to be within your own reach.'

Marcus Aurelius, *Meditations* 6.19

My parents always told me that I couldn't do DIY: 'Tim's good academically, just don't ask him to change a plug!'

The problem is that when we come to believe these stories – as we often do – they become self-limiting beliefs. There is a better way to think about your limitations.

Instead of saying 'I can't do it' – arguing for your limitations – try saying 'I can't do it … *yet*'.

The other day, our kitchen sink became blocked. My first reaction, based on my childhood script, was to call a plumber. Then I remembered Marcus's words. Just because it seemed difficult to me didn't mean it was impossible.

I found an instructive YouTube video relating to a similar problem. Thirty minutes later, the sink was unblocked.

It made my day. Not only had I saved some cash, but I'd also overcome a self-limiting belief!

169   Conquer yourself first so you can conquer the world

> 'People conquer the world by conquering themselves.'
>
> Zeno of Citium

As Zeno knew, courage is an inside job. It is often our own beliefs that limit us more than external obstacles.

When you find it difficult to make a start or feel like giving up, tell yourself: *This thought is just an impression in my mind and not an objective fact like it claims to be.*

For example, if you plan to go to the gym but then think, 'I don't feel like it today', you can challenge that thought by reminding yourself how you will feel after you have been.

If you feel like giving up on an important project, remember other times that you have succeeded in the past despite similar doubts. View this challenge as your chance to shine.

What is one of your self-limiting beliefs?

170   She moves in purpose-filled ways

From Sylvia Pierce – Life University women's wrestling athlete and influencer

I'm currently attending university on a wrestling scholarship. I wasn't always a champion, though. The early years on the mat were filled with heart-breaking losses. Trying to prove my abilities while overcoming gender stigma became an uphill battle, one that I nearly gave up. Then, in grade 10, I came across something Marcus Aurelius said. To paraphrase:

'Stop being aimless, stop allowing fears and anger to lead you astray. Instead, focus on doing what has to be done right now willingly, with precision, seriousness, and integrity. Free yourself from distractions. You can do it, if you approach each task as if it were your last.'

Meditations 2.5

The most distracting things were what others thought, something I couldn't control. I should only be proving myself to me. Popular opinion is nothing to me on the mat, and if I'm serious, I should only consider my form.

Marcus's words had a profound effect. Now I make sure every move I make is filled with purpose, on and off the mat … as if it were the last thing I was ever going to do.

171   There's no such thing as failure

When asked by a journalist how he'd coped with failing in his first 10,000 attempts to invent the light bulb, Thomas Edison responded, 'I hadn't failed. I had just found 10,000 ways that won't work.'

Edison displayed what modern psychologists call the 'growth mindset'. People with the growth mindset don't classify a negative outcome as a failure. They see it as part of the process towards success.

Or, as Winston Churchill is often quoted as saying, 'Success is stumbling from failure to failure with no loss of enthusiasm.'

172   Your secret weapon

The Stoics emphasized that our highest power is that of *rationality* – the ability to analyse situations logically. The next time you are held back from doing something that matters, ask these questions:

1. What is the worst outcome? Would that really be so bad? How could I deal with it, Stoically?

2. What is the best outcome? How would I feel then?

3. What is the most likely outcome?

Try out these three questions – your secret weapon against exaggerated fears.

173   Stoicism for social anxiety

'A lute player when he is singing by himself has no anxiety, but when he enters the theatre, he is anxious even if he has a good voice and plays well on the lute; for he not only wishes to sing well, but also to obtain applause: but this is not in his power.'

Epictetus, *Discourses* 2.13.1

The Stoics were so ahead of their time! Recent research by Clark and Wells (1995) has led cognitive behavioural therapists to recommend what Epictetus was suggesting nearly two thousand years ago!

So, when I advise clients to focus on their own performance and not what other people are thinking, I am echoing Epictetus.

Where can you use Epictetus's sage advice? Playing a musical instrument? Giving a talk? Playing at sport?

In each case, remember that what audience thinks is out of your control, and so is nothing to you! Focus only on what you are doing.

174   Stoicism during a storm at sea

During a storm at sea, an unnamed Stoic philosopher turned a ghastly pale like everyone else on board. Someone called him out over this: 'Aren't you Stoics supposed to be fearless?'

'Not at all,' replied the Stoic, and referred his inquisitor to a passage in Epictetus:

> 'While everyone will get the impression that danger is at hand,
> the wise person will not assent to this impression.'

Sure, he turned pale – this was the automatic reaction over which he had no control – but crucially, he did not give assent to the idea that there was anything to be really scared of. That's why he did not panic as many others had.

You can't control your initial bodily sensations or initial automatic thoughts. But you can control your response to them.

We can become more courageous by not taking these initial automatic reactions too seriously, then taking a step back and deciding for ourselves whether there is really anything to be scared about.

175 The faulty smoke alarm

Imagine a smoke alarm that goes off every time the toast gets burnt. What would you do with that alarm?

Turn it off?

No, because then you wouldn't know when there was a fire!

Assess the situation and realize that it's just burnt toast and not a fire.

Exactly! That's the Stoic way – to treat the initial feelings and thoughts as information: that maybe there's danger, but maybe not.

I often use this analogy to help clients prone to anxiety become more courageous. They begin to see their anxious thoughts and sensations as being just like a faulty smoke alarm. They learn to take a step back and, usually, ignore it. Could this idea help you?

176 Relabel anxiety as excitement

How can you tell when you're anxious?

My heart starts to beat faster and I get butterflies in my stomach.

How can you tell when you're excited?

My heart starts to beat faster and I get butterflies in my stomach.

That's right.

Physiologically, excitement and anxiety feel identical. It's the stories we tell ourselves about the sensations that make us want to avoid or rush into something.

Here's how you can use this to be more courageous.

The next time you notice your heart beating fast and you are attempting something in line with your core values – like giving a public talk or asking someone out on a date – relabel that sensation as excitement.

Tell yourself: 'I'm excited about giving this talk or going on this date.'

It all comes back to Epictetus, doesn't it? People are disturbed not by things but by the views which they take of them.

177   The courage to get out of bed

'In the morning when you get up unwillingly, let this thought be present – I am rising to do the work of a human being.'

Marcus Aurelius, *Meditations* 5.1

It seems even Marcus Aurelius had problems getting up in the morning. Why? Because instant pleasure is attractive. For Marcus, huddling under the blanket and staying warm was pleasurable. This might be a challenge for you – or it might be watching too much Netflix or eating a cookie.

In the same passage, Marcus provides the answer: 'You can do better. You were born for action, not feeling good.'

So, the next time you feel like taking the easy option, ask yourself: 'Is this what I was born for?'

178   The courage quotient quiz

There have been many courage tips in this chapter. You may recall the courage quotient mentioned in **157**:

Courage equals *willingness to act* divided by *fear*.

■ Which of these ideas we've talked about in this chapter can help you reduce fear (F)?

■ Which directly increase willingness to act (W)?

■ Which do both (B)?

We've done the first one, so you get the idea.

Entry	Tip	F (reducing fear) W (increasing willingness to act) B (Both)
156	Just do the right thing, now.	W
158	Stand up for your beliefs.	
159	Be indifferent to what makes no difference.	
161	What awkward questions would Socrates ask you?	
162	Cato telling you, 'You gotta do the right thing.'	
167	Recall your past successes.	
168	Overcome self-limiting beliefs.	
170	See challenges as your chance to shine.	
172	Analyse your fears logically.	
173	Focus on what you can control, not what others are thinking.	
175	Remember the faulty smoke alarm.	
176	Relabel anxiety as excitement.	

179   Courage quotient quiz answers

Here's my answer to 178:

Entry	Tip	F (reducing fear) W (increasing willingness to act) B (Both)
156	Just do the right thing, now.	W
158	Stand up for your beliefs.	W
159	Be indifferent to what makes no difference.	F

161	What awkward questions would Socrates ask you?	W
162	Cato telling you, 'You gotta do the right thing.'	W
167	Recall your past successes.	B
168	Overcome self-limiting beliefs.	B
170	See challenges as your chance to shine.	B
172	Analyse your fears logically.	F
173	Focus on what you can control, not what others are thinking.	F
175	The faulty smoke alarm.	F
176	Relabel anxiety as excitement.	B

Take a moment to reflect on which of these ideas works best for you.

180   Stoic encouragement

I hope that you find all the entries in this chapter encouraging.

Encouragement gives us courage.

You can gain further encouragement by reciting or memorising Stoic quotations – just like Uber whistleblower Susan Fowler.

You've already come across many encouraging Stoic sayings in this chapter. Here are some more:

> 'Be like the headland on which the waves continually break, but it stands firm.'
>
> Marcus Aurelius, *Meditations* 4.49

> 'How long, then, will you put off thinking yourself worthy of the highest improvements and follow … reason?'
>
> Epictetus, *Handbook* 51

'Don't put anything off. Balance your books
with life each day.'

Seneca, *Letters* 101

Memorize your favourite encouraging Stoic quotations so they are
ready at hand when you need them.

Follow-up

■ Retake the courage self-check-in (**152**).

■ The essential entry in this chapter is **156: The Stoic shortcut
to courage**.

■ How can you build on your courage challenge (**165**)?

CHAPTER 7
JUSTICE

Please do not be put off by the title of this chapter! It's not about the legal system, and it's only partly about the idea of fairness. For Stoics, justice is all about the way that you relate to other people. So, in this chapter, you'll be discovering Stoic ways to be a better friend, parent and citizen of the world. You will also be learning about important virtues related to justice such as gratitude, forgiveness, benevolence and compassion.

The Stoic who gives us our organizing framework is a little-known Stoic named Hierocles, who lived in the second century CE, after the 'big three' Stoics (Seneca, Epictetus and Marcus Aurelius) with whom we are more familiar.

Hierocles asks us to imagine ourselves surrounded by a series of concentric circles, the innermost of which contains our family, the outermost being the whole world. We should, says Hierocles, contract the outer circles so that we are as concerned for them as we are for ourselves. Far from seeing ourselves as an island, as the misinformed caricature has it, Stoicism challenges us to extend our care widely and ultimately to be a citizen of the whole world – a cosmopolitan.

181   What is justice?

You might think of justice as being about keeping to the law. Or maybe you equate it with fairness. For the Stoics – and for us in this chapter – justice is much broader and much more widely relevant. Justice includes positive qualities like love, kindness, forgiveness, gratitude, benevolence and compassion as well as fairness.

Rate yourself from 0 (very low) to 5 (very high) on the following qualities:

1. Being fair

2. Being kind

3. Being forgiving

4. Being grateful

5. Being compassionate

6. Being loving

7. Being benevolent

Which qualities would you like to score higher in?

182   Why is justice good?

Parents, teachers, priests and Stoic philosophers tell us to be fair, loving and kind – but why should we?

Clearly, it's in our interests for *other people* to be fair, loving and kind to us. But wouldn't the best idea be to encourage others to adopt this policy while we (secretly) pursue our own narrow self-interest?

What do you think?

Jot down the pros and cons of you being more just – remembering that in this chapter, and for Stoics, justice includes all the qualities mentioned in **181**.

183   The Stoic's motivation for being good to others

One very tempting answer to the question 'Why bother with justice?' is to do with reciprocity, summed up by the saying: 'You scratch my back, and I will scratch yours.'

Seneca said:

'If you want to be loved, love.'

Letters 9

Or, as The Beatles put it, 'The love you take is equal to the love you make.'

Reciprocity isn't an unjust motivation for being good to others. However, the Stoics believe that being *intrinsically* motivated to treat others fairly – without reward – is not only virtuous but also contributes to our long-term happiness. This is because it is in our nature to be social beings.

> 'You must live for another if you wish to live.'
>
> Seneca, *Letters* 48

Or, as modern-day Stoic and co-author of *The Good Life Method*, Dr Paul Blaschko, said, 'If you want to live a good life, learn to love the truth. Develop the ability to connect with other people and build true friendships and community, and to ask hard questions about what matters most in life.'

We are meant to live together and support each other. If we do not, we will not be living a good life and we will not flourish.

Do something to support your family member or co-worker today – and pay attention to the feeling of personal satisfaction it brings you.

184   Like a vine producing grapes ...

There is a fantastic passage in *Meditations* which puts the Stoic rationale for concern for others beautifully:

> There are some, who, when they have done you a favour, charge it to your account, as a great obligation. Others don't charge you, yet secretly look upon you as much indebted to them ... A third sort seem not to know what they have done; but are like the vine, which produces its bunches of grapes, and seeks no more when it has yielded its proper fruit. The horse, when she has run her course, the hound, when he has followed the track, the bee, when it has made its

honey, and the person, when they have done good to others, don't make a noisy boast of it, but go on to repeat the like actions, as the vine in its season produces its new clusters again ...'

Marcus Aurelius, *Meditations* 5.6

It's worth rereading this passage a couple of times.

Which of the three types of people mentioned by Marcus would you like to be?

185   Hierocles' Circles of Concern

Hierocles, a Stoic who lived in the century after Marcus Aurelius, asks us to imagine a series of concentric circles as illustrated below.

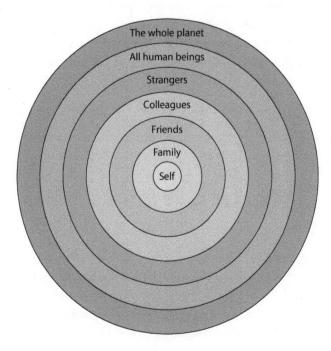

The whole planet
All human beings
Strangers
Colleagues
Friends
Family
Self

We are to imagine *ourselves* in the centre.

The next circle contains those we are closest to – our family. After this comes a circle including our friends and extended family. Surrounding this is a circle containing our work colleagues, neighbours and acquaintances.

Next come strangers, people in our country whom we've never met and who may be of a different social class and race. The penultimate circle includes strangers from other countries. Some modern Stoics have suggested we add a further circle, to include the whole planet – animals and the environment. I like this Modern Stoic innovation!

We should, says Hierocles, aim to bring the outer circles closer towards us. Ultimately, we can aim to take care of everyone with the same concern we would like for ourselves. Hierocles says a good start is treating people as if they were in a closer circle than where you would have originally placed them. For instance, you could care for a stranger as you would a work colleague. Or treat a distant relative as familiar as your own self, picking up the phone and offering them words that encourage the peace and preservation you would feel after exercising self-care.

Today, choose one circle to which you would like to extend your concern.

Make a conscious effort to treat the people in that circle as you would someone closer to your heart.

186   Rob expands his Circles of Concern

Rob finds the idea of expanding his circle of concern exciting.

Rob hadn't spoken to a friend since they graduated from high school, having gone off to different colleges. This was the longest they had gone without speaking and Rob felt he should expand his circle of concern despite the countless other things he had to worry about. He's glad he took the time because he found his friend at the lowest he'd ever been.

He was sure his friend appreciated the call.

What he never found out was that he actually saved his friend's life just by showing him that someone cared.

Is there anyone you could reach out to today?

187   Circles of Concern check-in

We will be using Hierocles' Circles of Concern as a framework throughout this chapter. In addition to extending your concern outwards, we will be checking whether you give each area sufficient care. So where are you now?

For each of the circles rate yourself out of 5, where 0 is lowest, 5 is highest.

1. Care for yourself

2. Care for your immediate family

3. Care for friends (and extended family)

4. Care for colleagues (and neighbours)

5. Care for strangers in your country

6. Care for all human beings

7. Care for animals and the environment

Add up your total score – from 0 to 35 (35 is highest).

Rate yourself today, then see whether your score has improved at the end of the chapter!

188   Being a good friend to yourself

The circles of Hierocles assume you take good care of yourself.

Do you?

Unfortunately, my experience as a therapist suggests that many people do not care for themselves properly.

What kind of relationship do Stoics think we should have with ourselves?

Seneca says we should

> **'be a friend to ourself.'**

Letters 6

What can you do, today, to be a better friend to yourself?

189 The oxygen mask

Some people believe that it's selfish to care for themselves. If you are one of these people, then it might help to recall the safety announcement they make in aeroplanes. You know, the one that goes: 'Should the cabin lose pressure, oxygen masks will drop from the overhead area. Please place the mask over your own mouth and nose before assisting others.'

Why do they say this? Surely, if you are travelling with little ones, you should put on their masks first?

Not at all, because you won't be much use to anyone if you suffocate.

To help others, you often need to attend to your own needs first.

190 The carers' dilemma

Brian and Judy have been looking after Judy's mother, whose early-stage dementia set in six months ago. It has put a great strain on their relationship.

What advice would you give Brian and Judy?

They will not be very effective support for Judy's mother if they are fighting or exhausted. They *both* need to put on their oxygen masks!

Flicking through *Meditations*, Judy comes across this statement:

'Don't be ashamed to be helped.'

7.7

She remembers a friend suggested arranging respite care for a weekend so that Judy and Brian could take a short break.

In the following weeks Brian, Judy *and* Judy's mother all feel the benefits.

The Stoics do indeed call for Judy to extend her concern towards her mother – but this needs to be done in a way that can be sustained, which means putting on her own oxygen mask first.

191   The fairness trap

There are several traps into which the unsuspecting novice Stoic can fall. One of the most common is what I have come to call 'the fairness trap'. It goes something like this:

'Fairness is part of justice, right? So, I must make sure that everyone is fair to me.'

Wrong.

There are at least four reasons why it's unhelpful to demand that others treat you fairly:

1. You can't control other people.

2. You need to focus on your own attitudes and actions, which you can control.

3. Thinking about things in this way will most likely make you less understanding (see **195** and **196**).

4. Stoics don't see relationships as being transactional (**183**, **184** and **185**).

Instead of demanding that others be fair to you, follow the wise advice of Marcus Aurelius:

'The one thing valuable in this life, is, to spend it in a steady course of truth, justice and humanity, towards even the false and unjust.'

Meditations 6.47

192   Look at things the right way

You may remember the Epictetus quotation about everything having two handles (76). Do you know how it continues?

Here's the passage in full:

'Everything has two handles: one by which it may be carried, another by which it cannot. If your brother acts unjustly, don't lay hold on the action by the handle of his injustice, for by that it cannot be carried; but by the opposite.'

Handbook 43

What Epictetus means is that there are two ways of looking at the issue. You could look at it in terms of your brother being unjust – but, for the reasons we've just mentioned (191), this would be a mistake. So instead, remember that he is your brother, and your relationship is unconditional, not transactional.

Of course, if we remember Hierocles and his Circles of Concern, we should be aiming to treat *everyone* as a brother.

193   Treat everyone like a brother

Marcus Aurelius says:

'We are made for co-operation, like feet, like hands, like eyelids, like the rows of the upper and lower teeth. To act against one

another then is contrary to nature; and it is acting against
one another to be vexed and to turn away.'

Meditations 2.1

Treat everyone like a brother – even if they are not literally your brother
and even if they are being unjust.

194   Forgiveness

'It is peculiar to man to love even those who do wrong.
And this happens, if when they do wrong it occurs to
you that they are kinsmen, and that they do wrong
through ignorance and unintentionally ...'

Marcus Aurelius, *Meditations* 7.22

Which of these do you think are the three *best Stoic* reasons for being
forgiving?

1. It will bring us closure.

2. People do wrong through ignorance.

3. Wrongdoings are often unintentional.

4. We are made for co-operation, not to be angry with each other.

The answer is 2, 3 and 4.

Marcus Aurelius practised what he preached, forgiving his co-general
who plotted against him.

What about forgiveness bringing about closure? Recent research (for
example, Worthington, 2020) endorses this view. Forgiveness benefits
the forgiver, as they lose bitterness and hatred. Stoics would count this
as a bonus, but not as their source of motivation to forgive. We should
forgive because it is just.

Do you want to choose to forgive someone, today? Who would that be?

195   Put yourself in their shoes

> 'I myself have done or might have done this very thing which
> I am angry with another for doing.'
>
> Seneca, On Anger 3.12

A father (whom I shall call Raymond) was becoming increasingly upset and frustrated with his young son. Instead of studying, all his son seemed to want to do was play video games. Raymond took this to mean that his son was lazy and disobedient.

Raymond started to see things differently when I asked him, 'What did you like doing when you were his age?' He remembered that he too had enjoyed video games very much. When he put himself in his son's shoes, he was able to see him in a different light – he was just being a boy, not particularly idle or rebellious.

Once freed from his unhelpful judgements, Raymond was able to think about more helpful ways to encourage his son to do his schoolwork – such as reading together in the evenings. Now that he was less frustrated, he was also better able to reconnect with his son, for example by playing football together – and his son started to do better at school!

196   Seek first to understand

> 'We have two ears and one mouth so we can listen twice
> as much as we speak.'
>
> Zeno of Citium

Are you someone who likes to talk and is always letting others know what you think? Or are you the kind of person who listens carefully to other people and asks questions so you can get to see their point of view?

Zeno, the founder of Stoicism, suggests the perfect ratio of listening to speaking – two to one.

Stephen Covey's writings are very consistent with Stoicism, and I find them helpful in working with relationships. 'Seek first to understand, and then to be understood' is his fifth habit of effective living.

If you don't understand someone's point of view, how can you know what matters to them or try to reach win–win agreements?

Marcus Aurelius said something very similar:

> 'Ensure that you attend exactly to what is said by others,
> and to enter into the mind of the speaker.'
>
> *Meditations* 6.53

Imagine Zeno is watching you today and remember that you have two ears and one mouth for a reason!

197 Make a deposit into your emotional bank account

One of Stephen Covey's most practical ideas is that of imagining an emotional bank account.

The idea is that your relationships can be either in the black or in the red. It's helpful to think about whether you are making a deposit or withdrawal when you interact with people.

For example, John's partner has had a tough week. She makes it clear that she would like a nice quiet weekend rather than the energetic, tiring weekend they had planned. John is initially irritated, as he had been looking forward to seeing friends and she had agreed to it, right?

He then considers his options through the lens of the emotional bank account. He could try to reach a compromise. But wouldn't this show lack of understanding and put the relationship in the red? Far better to agree gracefully to his partner's – quite reasonable – wishes.

What relationship can you improve today by making a deposit in the emotional bank account?

198   Be grateful

Many people are taken aback by the first book of Marcus Aurelius's *Meditations*, thinking it is just a laundry list of his tutors. But in fact, it's an expression of gratitude to those who have helped him.

Seneca also sees gratitude as an important quality:

> 'Let us, therefore, show how acceptable a gift is by loudly expressing our gratitude for it; and let us do so, not only in the hearing of the giver, but everywhere. He who receives a benefit with gratitude, repays the first instalment of it.'
>
> Seneca, *On Benefits* 2.22.1

I'd like to think that Marcus followed Seneca's advice and thanked many of these people in person or by letter. I expect he did.

Recent research (for example, see Emmons and Shelton, 2002) endorses the impact of gratitude on the giver as well as on the receiver. People were asked to write a letter of gratitude to someone who had helped them but whom they had not really thanked properly, and to arrange to deliver that letter *in person* and read it out to them. Both recipient and writer benefitted, and the relationship became stronger.

Martin Seligman, who wrote about this 'Gratitude Visit' exercise in *Authentic Happiness*, admits that this flies better in some cultures (USA) than in others (UK).

Be that as it may, why not be more grateful today?

199 Celebrate the success of others as if it were your own

> 'It's in keeping with Nature to show affection for our friends,
> and to rejoice in their advancement absolutely as
> if it were our own.'
>
> Seneca, *Letters* 109

How do you respond when a friend or relative has a success? Do you respond, as Seneca urges, enthusiastically? As if the success were your own?

Contemporary psychologist Shelly Gable has researched the impact on relationships of how we respond to their good news. Gable has found that those who embrace Seneca's advice and respond in what she calls an 'active and constructive' way improve relationships. Those who are uninterested ('What's on TV?') or negative ('That will mean longer hours, won't it?') damage their relationships.

Once again, the advice of the ancient Stoics is vindicated by modern research!

So, next time someone you know has a success, celebrate it as if it were your own.

200 Making progress

We begin life with an instinct for self-preservation – otherwise we wouldn't survive. As we get older, we form a natural affinity with those closest to us – usually our parents. As our rationality develops, we begin to realize that others are like us. We understand that others are worthy of care, just as we are. The further we progress rationally and ethically, the more consistently and fully we expand our care.

Does this sound at all like Hierocles' Circles of Concern? The Stoics called this process *oikeiôsis*.

Of course, not everyone progresses in this way, but that is usually because they have not been educated properly or have been corrupted by others. But all of us have the potential to get to the next level.

201   Do an evening review tonight

Whatever aspect of development you are working on, one of the most helpful tools in the Stoic toolkit is the evening review. To give you a kind of 'view from above' and check in how you are progressing as a Stoic, why not do an evening review based on the ideas expressed in this chapter?

Here's a recap on how you do it ...

Towards the end of the day, go through the day and ask yourself three questions:

1. What did I do well?

2. What could I do better?

3. What did I omit to do?

Today, do this while focusing on justice and how well you have acted with regard to other people.

202   Progressing by using the evening review

Jake is, to be frank, a little disappointed in himself after his evening review (201):

'I wake up with the best intentions but find myself reacting negatively far too often. I was particularly disappointed that I snapped at my 18-year-old son when he scratched the car.'

It's important to remember that the evening review is *not* about self-criticism so much as trying to be a better version of yourself next time.

Which of these Stoic ideas do you think Jake might find helpful?

1. Be forgiving rather than blaming.
2. Put yourself in the other person's shoes – you've made mistakes like this!
3. Avoid catastrophizing – it's only money.
4. You can't control what has happened, you can control your response.
5. Handle the situation in the right way – he is your son to whom you should be loving.
6. Remember that your response could put your emotional bank balance in either the red or the black.

203   Preparing yourself for a challenge

Jake thinks that all the ideas in 202 would have been helpful. He decides to use another Stoic tool, the premeditation of adversity (*premeditatio malorum*), to help him do better next time.

He replays the situation in his mind's eye. He is in the car with his son and hears the tell-tale scraping of metal against brick as the car scratches the gatepost.

He notices his impulse to curse his son, but instead takes it by the right handle – 'This is my son, and here is an opportunity to be loving, not chastising. How many times did I prang a car when I was young (and not so young …)? It's only money, and anyway I can't change the fact that it's scratched. Perhaps I should open the gate wider next time.'

Jake feels confident he would respond differently in this exact scenario. But how would he react to a different situation? His teenage daughter has been threatening to get a tattoo …

What interpersonal challenge could a premeditation of adversity help you with?

204 A citizen of the world

> 'I was not born in one corner, my country is the whole world.'
>
> Seneca, *Letters* 28.4

Following Socrates, the Stoics were among the first to propose that we should consider the whole of humankind to be our concern, not just those in our corner of the world.

As Epictetus put it:

> 'Do what Socrates did? Never in reply to the question, to what country do you belong, say that you are an Athenian or a Corinthian, but that you are a citizen of the world.'
>
> *Discourses* 1.9.1

What would you do differently today if you were to think of people in other corners of the world as worthy of your care?

205 Random acts of kindness

One of my favourite books is George Eliot's classic nineteenth-century novel *Middlemarch*. I find its final sentence to be particularly inspiring:

> '... the growing good of the world is partly dependent on unhistoric acts, and that things are not so ill with you and me as they might have been, is half owing to the number who lived faithfully a hidden life and rest in unvisited tombs.'
>
> Chapter 87

Every little bit helps.

One way to contribute is to practise random acts of kindness. Do something for the benefit of others, without expecting any reward. Examples include:

- Let someone out in front of you when driving.
- Give up your seat on a train or bus.
- Smile at strangers.
- Thank someone sincerely for something you appreciate.
- Donate to charity.
- Pick up litter.
- Be grateful.

Research suggests that doing random acts of kindness benefits the person doing them as well as those receiving them – even more if you do as many as five random acts of kindness in a single day.

How about making today the day for random acts of kindness?

206   Rational acts of kindness

I love the idea of random acts of kindness. Sometimes I wonder, though, if it would be even better to do *rational* acts of kindness. If I have £10 to give to charity, don't I want to give it to a charity that will use my £10 well, rather than waste most of it on administration?

Happily, an organization called Giving Well has done the research about which charities save or improve lives the most per pound – at the time of writing it's the Malaria Consortium (https://www.malariaconsortium. org/malaria/malaria_control.htm), which works to help stop the spread of malaria.

Another organization, 80,000 Hours (https://80000hours.org), offers free consultations for young people thinking about what career they can embark on to do the most good in the world, given their skills.

What would be the most *rational* act of kindness you would be willing to do today – the thing you could do that would make the biggest difference to the common good?

207   The Stoic gardener

From David Arnaud – retired academic who tries to grow as much of his own food as he can and still has hopes of perfecting his backhand at tennis

Five years ago, I started growing my own food in efforts to be self-sufficient. However, I've come to realize this is neither practical nor wholly worthwhile. Impractical, as I can't grow the variety of everything I'd like to eat, and not wholly worthwhile as it misses communality as something to be treasured. So, pure self-sufficiency turned out to be rather too egoistic a goal – both in the sense of being just about my food and work and as a failure to realize the important input of and connection with others.

What really matters besides the individual benefits of health and contact with nature is community and increasing the world's sustainability. So rather than growing food for myself, I'm growing food for many (lots of gluts to share), gardening regeneratively copying the methods nature herself uses, with no dig and food forest techniques which increase soil health and sequester carbon dioxide, and offering and receiving support from friends and neighbours – and writing this to encourage you.

208   The wider world of the Stoic

From Kai Whiting – researcher and lecturer in sustainability and Stoicism, co-author of *Being Better: Stoicism for a World Worth Living In* and co-founder of *Wisdom Unlocked*

Stoicism has helped me think about the wider world, in particular our obligations to each other, animals and plants. Stoicism is often seen as an internalized self-help philosophy, but it's very much more one of seeking harmony with the world around us. Stoicism has made me think deeply about climate breakdown, biodiversity loss and intergenerational injustice. It hasn't given me all the answers, but it has helped me ask better questions.

To find out more about Kai's work, go to https://wisdomunlocked.org

209   Doing better

From Greg Lopez – co-author *of Live Like a Stoic*, co-founder of The Stoic Fellowship, and member of the Modern Stoicism team

I've had first-hand experience seeing how people typically die in modern Western societies. I lost my parents at a young age from cancer and saw patients towards the end of their lives in hospitals while on rotation as a pharmacy student. Often, the way people go isn't great.

While other countries, like Switzerland and Canada, allow medical aid in dying to stop the suffering of people who are ill, the United States has much more limited options, including my supposedly progressive home state of New York, which is woefully behind in compassionate end-of-life care. Stoicism has helped me consistently push my representative to co-sponsor legislation over the years, even if the going is slow. I'd like to think this is Stoic resilience put to proper use: not just to *feel* better, but to help motivate me to *do* better.

210   The Circles of Concern morning meditation

Start the day right with this inspiring morning meditation:

1. Get comfortably seated and make sure you are in a quiet space for about five minutes.

2. Keep your eyes open, and look at the Circles of Concern diagram (185).

3. Begin with yourself, in the centre – are you taking sufficient care of yourself? What might you need to do to expand care for yourself? Perhaps you might decide to get out in the open air, seek physical restoration, or speak particularly kindly to yourself. Now imagine doing each of these things.

4. Next, move to your immediate family. Is there any relationship there that you would like to improve? How could you do that? Pause for a few seconds as you plan what you might do today.

5. Now think about your close friends and extended family. How are these relationships going? Who might benefit from you reaching out to them?

6. Next, think about work colleagues, neighbours and other people you might meet today. What can you do today to be kind and fair to them? In your mind, run through how you can achieve this today.

7. Now move on to strangers, people in other towns, and then in other countries. How could you extend your care to them?

8. Finally, think about the whole planet – the environment and all the creatures in it. What's bad for the planet is bad for everyone. Is there anything you can do today to show your care for the whole planet?

9. Take another look at the Circles of Concern diagram. If you found concern for *everyone* overwhelming, remember that it's OK to work on one circle at a time. Make a conscious decision to carry forward at least one of the ideas from the meditation. Congratulate yourself on spending this time on working on your own development, your own *oikeiôsis*.

Follow-up

■ Retake the self-assessments (181 and 187) and compare your old and new scores.

■ The essential entry in this chapter is 185: Hierocles' Circles of Concern.

■ Create ripples of kindness by sharing an idea from this chapter.

CHAPTER 8
WISDOM

Wisdom is the most important virtue.

Other virtues are applications of wisdom in different areas. Courage is applying wisdom in the face of danger, justice is wisdom when dealing with other people, and self-control is wisdom with respect to desires. All the virtues are wisdom, in a sense.

That's not all.

How do you decide which virtue you need? *Wisdom*.

How do you decide which virtue should take priority? *Wisdom*.

How do you select between externals? *Wisdom*.

How do you distinguish between what you can and cannot control? *Wisdom*.

That's why wisdom is the master virtue.

The question then becomes: 'How do I become wise?'

One way is to observe how people you would call wise behave and learn from them. We'll be looking at examples of Stoic sages and how to learn from them. Another great idea is to work through dilemmas, which also we'll be doing. I've compiled my top ten tips for wise Stoic decision-making to provide further assistance.

If you think that wisdom is something too grand, or beyond your reach, don't worry. The type of wisdom we are developing in this chapter is very practical. Don't worry if you don't yet feel sure in your knowledge. Socrates said he knew only one thing, that he knew nothing! Now we uphold him as one of the wisest men ever.

211 Wisdom quiz

1. The Greek for philosophy, *philosophia*, literally means 'love of …'?

2. The four cardinal virtues are courage, justice, self-control and …?

3. The Stoic sage is someone who has attained …?

4. The master virtue in Stoicism is …?

5. Who said, 'As you get older, three things happen. The first is your memory goes, and I can't remember the other two'? (*Clue: English comedian, first name Norman.*)

I'm sure you realized that the answer to each question is *wisdom* but how soon did you get that? Kudos to anyone who guessed before question 3!

212 The Stoic sage

Who would you pick as your ideal advisor, the 'sage on your shoulder'?

Your favourite Stoic? Marcus Aurelius, Epictetus, or Seneca?

Someone famous? Perhaps Nelson Mandela, Brené Brown or Greta Thunberg?

A fictional character? Yoda or Dumbledore would be good choices.

Someone you know? Maybe a teacher, grandparent or friend?

Who would you like to imagine whispering wise Stoic advice in your ear when you need it?

Have your personal sage on call today.

213 Socrates, a Stoic sage

'Socrates said, "We ought not to live a life without examination."'

Epictetus, *Discourses* 3.12

Had the ancient Stoics voted for their favourite sage, Socrates would have romped home.

Why was Socrates thought to be so wise?

He possessed insight into life and what was good. He was the first Greek philosopher to argue that wisdom is all you need to be happy.

Did Socrates also possess good judgement and act wisely?

Yes! Socrates embodied all the virtues. We've mentioned Socrates and his courage before. Even in his final days, in prison, he remained virtuous. He decided he would not attempt to escape, because it was the wrong thing to do and would make matters worse for those he cared about. It takes great strength of character to maintain virtue in the face of mockery, assault and imprisonment. This is why the Stoics look to his example often.

What's more, Socrates aimed at the common good and considered himself a citizen of the world, not just Athens. He tried to help people through what is now called 'Socratic dialogue' – asking people good questions so they could work towards more truthful conclusions.

Socrates was the epitome of wisdom.

Could Socrates be your sage?

214   What is wisdom? A Socratic dialogue

Pupil: I know! Wisdom is knowledge.

Socrates: What if I knew 50 words for snow – would that make me wise?

Pupil: No, you might win a quiz but that's not wisdom – wisdom is useful knowledge.

Socrates: What if I knew how to change a fuse – that could be useful – would that make me wise?

Pupil: Not exactly – to be wise you have to know about the really important things in life.

Socrates: What if I know those things yet do stupid or bad things?

Pupil: I'd expect a wise person to act wisely and ethically most of the time.

Socrates: So is wisdom insight into the things that matter in life and correspondingly good judgement and behaviour?

Pupil: Well, Socrates, that describes you – and you are the wisest person I know!

Socrates: Well, I wouldn't say that, but maybe we are both a bit wiser than we were at the start of this conversation.

215   What's your superpower?

If you could choose to have any superpower, what would it be? The ability to fly? Read minds? Time travel?

Flying? Didn't work out too well for Icarus and Daedalus …

Reading minds? Do you really want to know what everyone thinks about you?

Time travel? So your grandparents don't meet?

The point is, all powers are potentially problematic. The greater the power, the more dangerous, unless you use it well.

And what is the name of the quality that enables you to use other powers well?

Wisdom – it's a superpower.

If you find yourself feeling at all powerless today, remember that it's just your perspective, and not reality. You have all the power within you: *wisdom*.

216   Practical philosophy

How many philosophers does it take to change a light bulb?

None – they are too busy debating what the word 'change' really means.

Unfortunately, *modern* professional philosophy has a not entirely unjustified reputation for impracticality.

But the *ancient* philosophy we are looking at, Stoicism, is *very* practical.

Why?

Becoming more Stoic helps you become wiser – and wisdom is extremely practical. *And you'll still be able to change a light bulb!*

217   Serenity Prayer wisdom

Whenever I start dwelling too much on the past, Ravi is my personal sage. Ravi had been depressed for years and wasn't finding the CBT course I was running particularly helpful. Until we mentioned the Serenity Prayer.

A week later, Ravi looked an altogether different person.

He took out a drawing he had done. On the left side, he'd drawn a boggy field with grey clouds overhead. On the right, a green pasture bathed in sunshine. Separating them was a giant wall.

'The Serenity Prayer set off a light bulb in my mind. All these years I've been living in the wrong place in my head, dwelling on what's happened – that's the boggy field on the left. After hearing about the Serenity Prayer, I've realized I have a choice. For the last week, I've chosen to live more in the present. It's much brighter there! The wall stops me going back to the past.'

I noticed a small gap in the wall. 'What's that for?' I enquired.

'That's to remind me that if I ever find myself back in the past, I can always choose to return to the present.'

218 The three areas of study

The ancient Stoics divided philosophy into three areas of study – ethics, logic and physics. We've already covered a lot of this:

- *Ethics* includes knowing what is good and developing the virtues. Topics like happiness, finding the right direction, courage and justice reside under the umbrella of ethics.
- *Logic* involves good reasoning and helps us develop good judgement. Stoic serenity is rooted in this.
- *Physics* incorporates science and psychology as well as exploring philosophical questions (e.g. the existence of God) and gives us deep insight about life. The dichotomy of control falls into this camp.

You don't need to be a scholar to apply these studies to your life.

Choose one you feel resonates with you most and reflect on it throughout the day.

219 Living according to nature

The Stoics thought that happiness and wisdom were to be found by living according to nature. But what did they mean by this peculiar phrase?

First, it means living according to *human* nature. People have the capacity to reason, and live according to reason, which means using logic. It is also in our nature to be social beings and live up to our potential to progress ethically (*oikeiôsis*).

Second, it means living according to the *physical* laws of nature. Obviously, if you try to defy the law of gravity – for instance trying to fly unaided – your life will not go smoothly! Equally, there are natural cycles such as birth and death, summer and winter. These are part of the natural order of things, not things to feel anguish about.

Do you fight the tide, causing unnecessary stress? Or do you live according to nature?

220   Going with nature's flow

My wife and I recently went for a walk in an Area of Outstanding Natural Beauty by the coast.

It was blissful. Birds were singing. The fresh sea air soothed us. We felt at one with nature and discussed moving there. We managed to savour the happy moments together.

Then along came a sudden downpour, which turned into a torrential storm. We had no shelter, and no option but to keep going. We retained our sense of humour, though, reminding ourselves of how we endured a worse storm years ago in Corsica. Eventually we arrived back at the car, drenched.

But it was fine.

It was all part of living in accordance with nature, understanding its cycles, its good and bad weather.

In life, it's OK to savour the 'good weather' if we don't expect it to last for ever. When bad weather comes, as it surely will, we can call upon our Stoic virtues like wisdom and courage to handle it with grace. Humour can be a useful tool as well. To paraphrase Seneca, laughing at life is better than moaning about it.

221   In praise of the Logos?

Have you ever wondered why there is something rather than nothing? Have you ever pondered questions like 'Why do the laws of physics appear to be exquisitely fine-tuned to allow for stable matter and objects like galaxies, stars and planets to exist – and ultimately for life to exist?' or 'How can we puny humans survive in a world containing much stronger predators?'?

Me neither!

But the Stoics thought deeply about such questions. Surely, something had to make the universe exist and operate the way it does. They called this force Nature, God or the Logos. But the Stoics were pantheists, so they didn't think of God as being like the Christian God, a separate being apart from everything else. No, this universal force they considered the animator *in* everything, the orchestrator of growth both in people and the planet. This force must be providential for there to be something rather than nothing and matter to be stable. Of all creatures, human beings alone are infused with a spark of the Logos – our reason – and this enables us to survive and, potentially, flourish.

Some of these ideas from Stoic physics may sound rather strange. But don't you agree that it is equally strange – and wonderful – that there is something rather than nothing? That matter is stable and has woven itself into life and that we puny humans managed to survive and indeed thrive?

222   *Amor fati*

'Demand not that events should happen as you wish; but wish them to happen as they do happen, and you will go on well.'

Epictetus, *Handbook* 8

Amor fati (Latin for 'love of fate') means embracing your fate, however bad it seems.

Pollyanna gave positive thinking a bad name. When as a girl she was given a pair of crutches instead of the doll she longed for, her father invented 'the glad game' to pacify her. Whatever happens, you find a reason to be glad. 'It's good I got crutches, so I can appreciate not needing them.'

But for the Stoics, *amor fati* is no game. Given that Nature (or God) is good, it's *logical* to believe that everything is for the best. Sometimes, when we see the big picture, we understand that apparently bad things are for the best. But the universal force works in mysterious ways. So, even when we can't see why an apparent calamity is good, we should trust Nature and welcome it.

As the early Greek Stoic Chrysippus quipped: the foot, if it had intelligence, would willingly get muddy.

223   *Amor fati* in practice

Ireland is a wonderful country, but it's very wet! I recall a childhood holiday when we drove hours to the one place forecast to be dry – and it poured down there, too!

Max emigrated to Ireland from Australia to be with the girl he loved. He also liked the beer and the lush, green countryside. He hated the weather, though. Why couldn't it be sunny like in his native Brisbane? Then one day the truth dawned on Max:

The countryside is so green and beautiful because of all the rain! The rain and the green fields are two sides of the same coin!

From that day onwards, Max came not just to *accept* the rain but to *welcome* it.

Even his foot, if it had intelligence, would have volunteered to get muddy!

224 Stoicism and the environment

> 'What's bad for the hive is also bad for the bee.'
>
> Marcus Aurelius, *Meditations* 6.54

A hive is a complex, interactive system, which flourishes because each bee plays its part well. The universe is also a complex, interacting system in which we have an important part to play.

Yet we can be like thoughtless students sharing a house, trashing the place knowing that they will soon move on. Or we can be thoughtful custodians of planet Earth, doing our best for future generations.

> 'Can't you see the little plants, little birds, ants,
> spiders and bees working together to put in order
> their part of the universe?'
>
> Marcus Aurelius, *Meditations* 5.1

Can you be like them?

Be mindful of your part in caring for the planet, playing your role as well as you can today.

225 Virtue ethics

How do Stoics decide what to do?

Some ethical theories suggest we should follow simple rules like 'Never lie'. But what if telling a lie meant saving the life of an innocent person? Stoics understand that context is key, and rules are better understood as *guidelines*.

Other philosophies recommend calculating consequences and doing whatever seems best for the common good. But this assumes superhuman powers of knowledge and impartiality. Stoics care about consequences and are concerned about the common good, but don't expect people to perform mathematical calculations to optimize every action.

Stoicism is a form of virtue ethics, which, arguably, combines the best features of other theories. When deciding what to do, Stoics look at the situation through the lens of the virtues, aiming to do what the virtuous person (the sage) would do.

Where have you applied virtue ethics so far in your everyday life?

226   What would a Stoic do?

A great way to become wiser is to reflect upon an ethical dilemma. It's what doctors do as part of their training.

Here are four such dilemmas. What should a Stoic do?

1. Your ex-partner is in the catchment area of the best school. Your child lives with you, though, and you aren't. You consider fibbing about their residence. Should you?

2. A relative is leading a very unhealthy lifestyle and is resistant to change. Should you convince them to change or should you accept it's beyond your control?

3. Your company is struggling in the recession. Should you consider redundancies?

4. An aggressive drunk spits in your face. How should you react?

The next four entries might help you decide.

227   'I just want the best for my kids ...'

Isn't it OK to fib and pretend your child lives with you to get them into a better school – it's for the sake of your child, right?

Not according to Epictetus (*Handbook* 34). He says that if you can help others and keep your own honour and virtue, then fine – otherwise not. Would it be fair to the child whose place your child would take? Would you want your child to have to lie about where they live?

The dichotomy of value gives the same answer. Your good character trumps the benefits of a better school, such as higher grades.

A Stoic would consider how to get their child a good education while keeping their honour, such as moving into the catchment area themselves. In this case, they would not need to lie.

228   Intervention or acceptance?

A relative is leading a very unhealthy lifestyle and is resistant to change. Should you convince them to change or should you accept it's beyond your control?

Marcus Aurelius provides the answer:

> 'If you can, change them by teaching, but if you cannot,
> remember that kindness was given to you for this.'
>
> *Meditations* 9.11

If your relative's lifestyle is objectively harmful then you *should* try to convince them. But you should not expect immediate results. Keep trying and be kind. Like the Stoic Archer, do not blame yourself – or them – if you don't get the desired outcome. Ultimately, you can't make them change, but you can cultivate justice to attempt, courage to persist, self-control to manage frustration and wisdom to do your best, skilfully.

229   Tough decisions

From Justin Stead – CEO of Radley and founder of The Aurelius Foundation

Over the course of my career, unforeseen global events (the financial crisis of 2007 and the COVID-19 pandemic in 2020) had a profoundly negative impact on my international businesses. Would they survive such a disruptive financial storm?

Unfortunately, very difficult decisions had to be made to ensure the businesses could survive and inevitably this involved a restructuring process. The objective was to save the majority of the team so we were forced, very sadly, to let some people go – without question, this was the most heart-breaking part of a CEO's responsibility.

The Stoic mindset was important during these periods. It reminded us that acting on behalf of the greater good meant that the needs of the many had to prevail. We prioritized exercising compassion by assisting those we let go in finding new opportunities and providing other support mechanisms.

Tough decisions are often ill-timed, and their outcomes are not always preferred. I believe, however, Stoic Leadership, utilizing the four virtues, leads to the greater good being served on a consistent basis.

An understanding of Stoic Leadership can give CEOs the most rational and humane skill set to handle any situation, no matter how challenging.

230   Discretion is the better part of valour

From Walter J. Matweychuk – practising Rational emotive behaviour therapy (REBT) psychologist in Philadelphia, Pennsylvania. Visit REBTDoctor.com for more information

Thirty years ago, I found myself in a hot, crowded bar. Everyone was having a good time until a hulking man started pouring beer in his mug from unattended pitchers. When he arrived at mine, I snatched his wrist and said firmly, 'That is not yours!'

He spat in my face. Now I had to decide … respond with rage, or use good judgement? I'd spent five years finishing my doctorate dissertation, and suffering a head injury and being unable to make my oral defence the following week wasn't worth it.

So I took my glasses off and wiped them on my pants. As I silently left, I thought, 'Dirty water, just dirty water.' I went home to take a shower and have never regretted controlling what was under my control. Risking bodily injury would have been a foolish attempt at teaching virtue to a large, drunk man.

231 Caution – your internal hazard warning light

Would you have felt uneasy in any of those situations? If so, that's a *good* thing. Stoics called this feeling *caution*. It's a helpful emotion because it signals to you to reflect carefully about what to do. It's your internal hazard warning light.

You might call 'caution' something else – unease, worry, concern or your conscience.

When was the last time you experienced this feeling? Maybe when you hadn't contacted a friend in need or were considering alcohol when you had to drive home?

From today, start to notice this feeling and label it 'caution', because it will help you … well … be cautious.

232 Stoic guidelines for wise decision-making

Here are my top ten guidelines to help you make wise decisions:

1. Focus on what is up to you – your attitude and your actions.
2. Use a virtues lens – think about which virtues are most relevant.
3. Justice entails seeing things from others' point of view, thinking about your key roles and aiming for the common good.

4. Courage means doing the right thing even when it is difficult or risky.

5. Self-control means being moderate in your desire for any externals.

6. Do what virtue requires, even if this means forgoing externals like money, pleasure and status.

7. It's OK to select appropriate externals if it doesn't mean compromising on virtue.

8. Pick a 'sage on your shoulder' to help you decide what to do.

9. Like the Stoic Archer, try your best to achieve a good outcome but acknowledge that the outcome is beyond your control, while not placing blame.

10. Do a Stoic *premeditatio malorum* (premeditation of adversity – see 203) to prepare for possible setbacks.

Next time you are faced with a dilemma, see how much these guidelines help.

233   The wisdom of Solomon

Consider the dilemma faced by King Solomon.

Faced with two women who both claimed to be a baby's mother, he proposed cutting the baby in half. The real mother revealed herself by withdrawing her claim, to save the baby.

A virtuoso decision-maker like Solomon would have seen this instinctively. But we, who are still learning, need to reflect more deliberately. Run through the ten guidelines. Which help you come up with Solomon's solution?

Did you choose guideline 3 and see things from the perspective of both women?

Try to use these guidelines whenever you are faced with a dilemma.

With practice, you too can have the wisdom of Solomon.

234   My King Solomon moment

I wouldn't claim the wisdom of Solomon, but I have my 'King Solomon moments'.

My kids, then aged six and four, and I were returning home having had a great time at the park. But in a flash of insight, I knew there would be a big argument as they rushed in and fought to tell their mother about their adventures. How could I prevent this outcome?

'I see the future!' I announced dramatically. 'I see you both rushing to be the first to tell Mummy about your adventures. She's going to get annoyed with your squabbling. There will be tears … But wait … I see another future. You follow me quietly and take it in turns to tell Mummy. She shares your excitement!'

'Which future would you like?' I asked. 'It's up to you.'

'The first one!' replied my six-year-old cheekily.

But they entered quietly and calmly related their stories in turn.

Recall your own King Solomon moment, when your timely insight helped others.

235   Updating Stoicism?

Did you spot that elephant in the room? A big fat jumbo, with a banner over it saying 'STOIC PHYSICS' in large letters?

Stoic physics was based on an understanding of the world more than two thousand years ago. Haven't we learned quite a lot since then, some of which undermines the Stoic view? Can you provide a better explanation for some of the questions posed in 221? Quite possibly, but the Stoicism that emerges even if we don't rely on physics is still immensely powerful. We'll be thinking more on how much Stoic physics is valuable in Chapter 12. If you want to explore this topic in depth, I'd recommend *Stoicism: Cobwebs and Gems*, a book I've written with Chuck Chakrapani.

If you are reading Epictetus's *Handbook* and are put off by his references to God, soothsayers and suchlike – get hold of Massimo Pigliucci's excellent revisioning of Epictetus in the light of modern science. It's called *The Stoic Guide to a Happy Life*.

236   Modern Stoicism

'Shall I not go in the footsteps of those who came
before? I will indeed use the ancient road, but if
I find a better route, I will create a new one.
Our predecessors are not our masters,
but our guides.'

Seneca, *Letters* 33.11

In this book, I haven't been shy to include insights from psychology, psychotherapy and other disciplines, when they build on and enhance Stoic ideas.

We've drawn on CBT for tips on sleep, anxiety and mood management.

We've drawn on positive psychology to bolster ideas for self-control and courage.

In so doing, we are developing a *Modern* Stoicism. Since we know much more about the brain and what interventions work than even the wisest of ancient sages, this means that, as Seneca recommended, the ancient road is our guide but not our master.

Any other strategy would be folly.

237   Stoic WOOP

People sometimes ask whether Stoicism encourages positive or negative thinking. The simple answer is that Stoicism promotes the wise use of *both*. So does one of my favourite exercises from positive psychology.

It was developed by Dr Gabriele Oettingen and is called WOOP. It has four steps:

1. Wish – for a desired outcome.

2. Outcome – imagine the outcome vividly.

3. Obstacle – think of an obstacle.

4. Plan – to overcome the obstacle.

Do the last two stages remind you of the *premeditatio malorum*?

To make WOOP even more Stoic, be sure that your wish is in line with virtue and your key values and is under your control. For example, Grace has a work presentation tomorrow. Here's her Stoic WOOP:

Wish – *I want to do my best.*

Outcome – *I feel proud of myself.*

Obstacle – *Getting flustered.*

Plan – *Rehearse in front of mirror. Reread the chapter on Stoic serenity.*

How can *you* WOOP your way towards success?

238   Ulysses and the Sirens

'And though you are not yet a Socrates, you ought, however, to live as one seeking to be a Socrates.'

Epictetus, *Handbook* 51

> 'If you try to act a part beyond your powers, you not only
> disgrace yourself in it, but you neglect the part which you
> could have filled with success.'

Epictetus, Handbook 37

Is Epictetus contradicting himself?

No. You should *seek* to be a Socrates, but that doesn't mean that you imagine that you have all his virtues.

We all require self-knowledge – knowing our limitations and taking them into account.

Be like Odysseus (Ulysses), who was sailing past the island of the Sirens, whose enchanting songs lured sailors to their death. Odysseus desperately wanted to hear their music but knew that once he did he would lack the self-control to resist their lure. He told his crew to steer clear of the island whatever he later instructed. They were to stuff their ears with wax, so they couldn't hear the music. Odysseus was to be tied to the mast so he couldn't take control of the ship.

So Odysseus got to hear the Sirens' sweet songs and stay alive. He did this by understanding his own limitations, and wisely working around them to achieve his objectives.

239   The lawnmower story

One evening I returned from work, exhausted. I went straight to the couch, flicking through TV channels and contemplating a snack and a nap. But then a little voice urged caution: 'You know how this will end up; it's happened before. You will raid the sweets cabinet and spend the evening watching junk TV.'

What could I do instead? The answer was staring me in the face.

Through the French windows, I could see our lawn, getting out of control. I know from experience – *and from what I instruct clients!* – that the best way to beat mental fatigue is physical exercise.

But mowing the whole lawn seemed too daunting. Making a start was doable, though.

So, I got off my backside and started mowing. After a few minutes, I felt more energized, and mowed the whole lawn. Thirty minutes later, I was physically tired but mentally fresh – and proud of myself.

It wasn't difficult to mow the lawn, I just needed the wisdom to understand that I had to know my limitations and take that first baby step.

240   Learning to be wise

How could Stoicism help 26-year-old Guy, who works in advertising for an oil company but has grave reservations about the ethical impact of his work? He is passionate about photography.

Here are some ideas:

- *Virtues lens* – think about which virtues are most relevant:
    - *Justice* – it's not right to contribute to environmental damage.
    - *Courage* means having the guts to try to change jobs.
    - *Self-control* means accepting that he might have less money and it might take time.
    - The *dichotomy of value* means prioritizing virtue over externals.
- Guy might pick Alan Rickman as his *sage*, to remind him that career changes can work out. When he was Guy's age, Rickman had been a graphics designer. He became a jobbing actor, and much later found fame, playing Severus Snape in the *Harry Potter* movies.

- Like the Stoic Archer, Guy should take responsibility for doing his best but not blame anyone if it doesn't work out.

Guy's premeditation sees him quitting his job and struggling to find work in photography and not being able to pay his rent. So, he decides to find work for an ethical advertising agency, while doing a course in photography and building up a freelance photography practice.

Follow-up

- Have another go at **226**: What would a Stoic do?
- The essential entry in this chapter is **232**: Stoic guidelines for wise decision-making.
- Use these ideas to help you deal with a decision you are currently facing.

CHAPTER 9
COPING WITH ADVERSITY

'I did not think this would happen.'

'Would you ever have believed that this would happen?'

'But why shouldn't it?' answers Seneca (*Of Peace of Mind* 11).

We will all face crises and difficulties, which we will surely handle better if we are well prepared. This chapter will show you how.

A key idea is to mentally rehearse how you would deal with potential difficulties. In the same way that a pianist would prepare for a public concert by practising relatively easy pieces without an audience, we begin by considering relatively minor upsets – such as travel plans being disrupted – before moving on to more daunting misfortunes.

As well as the premeditation of adversity, we will be hearing about other helpful Stoic ideas, such as framing difficulties as Stoic opportunities, *amor fati* and 'the obstacle is the way'. Many of the Stoic tools you have already learned will also prove to be of great value.

Dealing with adversities can be tough.

Stoicism can help you make it through them.

241   The premeditation of adversity

> 'If you want someone to stay calm in a crisis, train
> them beforehand.'

Seneca, Letters 18.6

Self-help books often advise us to think positively. Yet bad things do happen, even to good people. If we rely exclusively on positive thinking, we will be surprised and, worse, unprepared.

The Stoic answer is to train yourself beforehand by carrying out regular premeditations of adversity. It's easy – there are just two steps:

1. Think of something that might go wrong – it's best to start with minor upsets.

2. Plan how you would cope well in that eventuality.

Try this one now.

Close your eyes and place yourself in this scenario for two minutes ...

You're in a crowded, bustling airport, and your flight has been delayed with no further updates.

What are your initial feelings? Angry? Wondering why they can't tell you what's going on? Anxiously thinking, 'What if I don't make my connection?'

Now, let's move on to developing your Stoic coping strategy.

242   Stoicism at the airport

From Phil Yanov – Founder of Tech After Five and a member of the Modern Stoicism team

As I write this, I am sitting inside, by its own claim, the world's busiest and most efficient airport. I've heard that announced on the overhead speaker several times by the mayor of the city in which I am stranded, Atlanta.

I'm on a family trip, a sometimes stressful event anyway, sitting at the wrong gate. The seating area of my proper gate is overflowing with stranded, cranky passengers.

You know what? It's OK.

While I have zero control over the weather, the airlines and my fellow passengers, I've got control over *me*. I know that I can choose how to respond. I love having that power, keeping my head when others are losing theirs. I think it makes me a better person, husband, father and citizen.

In this moment, I could be restless, complaining and cranky. Instead, I am doing what I was born to do. Better yet, in this moment, I am able to type out a few words to support Tim LeBon, someone I admire.

Earlier in the week, I asked my boy what I should write about. He said that he had often observed how practising Stoicism had helped me remain calm in some very trying circumstances.

If that were the only benefit I received from being a Modern Stoic, I'd be satisfied.

243 Your Stoic toolkit for coping with adversities

Did your premeditation of adversity resemble how seasoned Stoic Phil handled a similar situation? Here is a reminder of some key tools from the first three chapters, which form the building blocks of the Stoic approach:

- The *dichotomy of control* (Chapter 1) – control the controllables.
- *Virtues and the dichotomy of value* (Chapter 2):
  - Focus on what virtues you need.
  - Remember that a good character is all you need for a good life.
- The *STOIC way towards serenity* (Chapter 3), which includes:
  - challenging snap judgements
  - getting things in perspective
  - forgiveness, not blame, and
  - choosing the right way to handle things.

Take a couple of minutes and have another go at the premeditation of a long delay at the airport. How much better equipped to cope do you feel now?

244   Quick quiz

Gary has just been passed over for promotion. Which are considered Stoic responses?

   A 'This is a disaster. I will never achieve anything in life.'

   B 'That's disappointing, but maybe there's something I can learn from this. I will ask for feedback.'

   C 'It's only money and status, which won't make the real difference between me being happy or not.'

   D 'I've just got to suck it up.'

Answers? B, when Gary displays courage by asking for feedback, and C, where he considers the promotion a preferred indifferent.

In response A, Gary catastrophizes and buys into his snap judgements. In D, he acts as a lowercase stoic by repressing emotion instead of willingly accepting his fate and acknowledging what he can change.

245   Stoic tests and opportunities

> 'Difficulty shows people what they are. Therefore,
> when a crisis falls upon you, remember that you are as the
> raw youth with whom God the trainer is wrestling. Why?
> So that you may become an Olympic conqueror,
> but it is not accomplished without sweat.'
>
> Epictetus, *Discourses* 1.24

This is one of my very favourite Stoic ideas! Instead of being upset by something that happens, label it as a Stoic *test* or *opportunity*.

A Stoic test enables you to gauge how far you've come in your quest to become more Stoic.

A Stoic opportunity is a chance to hone and practise your Stoic skills.

So, next time something untoward happens – a noisy neighbour or a cold call perhaps – view it in a positive light.

See how many opportunities you can find today to practise Stoicism!

246   My Stoic test – getting COVID-19

Having dodged COVID-19 for 18 months, I finally got it – ironically, while writing this chapter! When I saw the positive test result, quite a few troubling thoughts crossed my mind:

'What if I get long COVID?'

'What if I infect the rest of my household?'

'I won't have time to meet my book deadline …'

I soon came to see even getting COVID-19 as a Stoic opportunity to practise using my toolkit.

How do you think Stoicism could help me dispel my concerns?

247   How did I do?

Once I took a step back and challenged my negative thinking, Stoicism, as usual, provided a helpful way forward. These were my answers to this particular 'Stoic test':

'What if I get long COVID?' *Don't catastrophize. You are vaccinated, and this is a milder strain. If you do get long COVID, you will cope with it.*

'What if I infect other members of my household?' *Use the virtues – especially wisdom. Self-isolate. Wear a mask – or two! – if you must be in the same room as them. If you do infect them, don't blame yourself. Like the Stoic Archer, you did your best.*

'I won't have time to meet my deadline.' *Catastrophizing again: you should only be out of action for a few days.*

My Stoic responses proved to be right on the money. I didn't get long COVID, I didn't infect anyone, and I met my deadline!

There was also an unexpected bonus from getting COVID. As a therapist, I frequently support patients who suffer from fatigue. Getting COVID-19 helped me empathize with their experience.

248   A Stoic test ...

From Dr Shamil Chandaria OBE – Senior Research Fellow, Centre for Eudaimonia and Human Flourishing, Linacre College, University of Oxford

As COVID-19 lockdown restrictions were slowly being lifted, I was finally able to go on the ten-day silent meditation retreat that I'd been looking forward to for the last year. Ten days of peace, silence, serenity and personal exploration – *ahhh, bliss.*

But when I arrived, I was informed that due to the enhanced hygiene and housekeeping protocols, we would all have to do two hours of cleaning duty. I was assigned scrubbing the dining hall, sweeping the floors, mopping, garbage, etc. My heart sank. My thoughts raced: *This is ridiculous. I'd very happily pay more to avoid this. Maybe I'll just leave!*

From the first day, I resented every task. I cringed as I sorted plastic and paper from soggy used tea bags. I felt nauseated at the stench of kitchen waste and rotting compost, and I tried to avoid breathing in the flying bugs. My aversion to the duties was palpable, and the net result was simple: I was suffering.

How do you think Shamil used Stoicism to help him turn this around?

249 ... becomes a Stoic opportunity

From Dr Shamil Chandaria

But as my duties ended that first day, it struck me that I had created my own little nightmare. Had I got this backwards? Perhaps these duties were a perfect opportunity to engage with as a meditation – after all, I was on a meditation retreat. Could I perform my duties with mindful attention, with equanimity? Could I perform my duties with wholesome acceptance?

Over the next days, whenever I noticed aversion creeping up, I reminded myself to take on the attitude of wholesome acceptance. With that change of attitude, a little Stoic alchemy started to happen. The tasks didn't feel so unpleasant.

As the days went on, another transformation started happening. I began to *enjoy* the tasks, I wanted to perform them as well as I could! I suddenly wanted to do my duties with diligence, taking pride in how clean the bins were after I sanitized them, and how spotless the floors were after mopping. This twist was the second phase to my Stoic alchemy! The unpleasant transmuted into pleasant into being a source of pride and accomplishment that results from performing them excellently. *Ha!*

250 Stoicism after a break-up

Linda's partner walked out on her and their baby, leaving her feeling betrayed and abandoned. A year later, she was alternating between revenge fantasies and trying to win him back.

Learning about the dichotomy of control was life-altering for Linda. It helped her fully understand that she absolutely could not control her ex. She had spent a year trying everything!

But she could take charge of her own life, because that was under her control. She stopped following her ex on social media and banished all thoughts of getting back together. This freed her up to focus her energy on doing things that would help her move on and nourish her, like taking up yoga.

Once Linda stopped trying to control what she couldn't, she noticed a dramatic improvement in her life.

251   Stoicism in a medical emergency

From Massimo Pigliucci – author of *How to Be a Stoic* and a member of the Modern Stoicism team

One fine morning in Brooklyn, New York, not long ago, I awoke with a mild fever. *Uh-oh*, I thought, *here comes COVID!* Turns out, it wasn't COVID, and even after spending three days in the ER, my doctors still don't know what it was. Most likely hypotheses: a mini-stroke or micro-seizure.

Either way, the scariest symptom was – fortunately transitory – an episode of aphasia. I knew that I wanted to write an email to my students to alert them that class was cancelled, but my brain just couldn't direct my fingers on the keyboard.

What got me through those three days, other than the love and support of my wife, was one of the most crucial and useful ideas in Stoicism: the dichotomy of control. Every now and then, at the hospital, I asked myself: *What, here and now, is up to me and what is not up to me?*

It was up to me to be nice to the doctors, nurses and fellow patients, as well as to co-operate to the best of my abilities with those trying to help me. Not up to me was everything else, including possibly surviving the experience.

I did survive it, and I am enormously grateful for it. Gratitude, too, is a crucial Stoic value.

252   Count your blessings

> 'Don't let your thoughts dwell upon what you want,
> so much as upon what you have.'
>
> Marcus Aurelius, *Meditations* 7.27

Many people poison their life by focusing on what they haven't got.

'Now that I'm old, I can no longer play tennis.'

'Having lost my job, I can't go on holiday.'

People compare their lives with what they would like them to be, then despair when they notice everything that's wrong. Instead of 'compare and despair', the Stoics recommend the opposite approach – gratitude and focusing on what you *have* got.

'Because of my body I can't play tennis, but thankfully I still have a good brain. I used to love playing chess – I will start playing again.'

'It's true, I haven't got enough cash to go abroad this year. But there are some amazing areas to explore closer to home – let's do that.'

By focusing on what you have, you replace a narrative that can lead only to depression and bitterness.

It was for this reason that Cicero said:

> 'For this one virtue [gratitude] is not only the greatest,
> but is the parent of all the other virtues.'
>
> *For Plancius* 80

Today, count your blessings, and focus on what you can do, not the things you can't.

253   Gratitude as a remedy for disappointment

From Ronald W. Pies – author of *Everything Has Two Handles: The Stoic's Guide to the Art of Living* and *The Three-Petalled Rose*, a book about the synthesis of Judaism, Buddhism and Stoicism

My wife and I had planned a trip to Turks and Caicos to celebrate our 25th wedding anniversary, but the trip had to be cancelled when the pandemic began. We were disappointed, but we accepted reality and rescheduled for eight months later. Unfortunately, the pandemic was still very widespread, and we had to cancel yet again.

My sense of disappointment was compounded by the sinking feeling that we might never make it to our island paradise. Logically, of course, we both knew better. We reminded ourselves of how well off we were, compared to so many suffering in the pandemic. At least we were alive, healthy and financially able to contemplate a vacation!

Marcus Aurelius begins his *Meditations* by voicing his gratitude to all those who helped shape his outlook on life, and Seneca calls upon us to cheerfully make the most of the things that come our way. Drawing on the important Stoic virtue of gratitude allowed my wife and me to regroup and move on – and yes, to reschedule. We're hoping third time's a charm!

254   Pain versus suffering

Karen Duffy ('Duff') has chronic sarcoidosis, a debilitating condition which causes chronic pain and impaired visibility, among other things.

Duffy has written a book, *Backbone*, in which through good humour and wisdom, she demonstrates the dictum that while pain is inevitable, suffering is optional.

Instead of complaining about all the things she can no longer do – like walking without a cane or having another child – she focuses on what she can do, including being a hockey mum and volunteering.

She says that Stoicism has been an inspiration to her and provided her with a moral compass.

Although she would not have chosen to have her chronic condition, her attitude towards it – and her Stoicism – have helped her grow as a person. It has, she concludes in the final sentence of her book, helped her to 'grow a backbone'.

255   The freedom to choose your attitude

Aspiring Stoics sometimes ask for book recommendations. As well as the Stoic classics, there's one book I suggest. It's written by someone who didn't identify himself as a Stoic but was clearly influenced by Stoicism: *Man's Search for Meaning* by Viktor Frankl.

The book describes the lessons he learned from years in Nazi concentration camps during the Second World War. In the camps, prisoners were stripped of almost everything. All that was left were naked starving people with a prison number. Viktor Frankl, up-and-coming Viennese psychiatrist, became prisoner 119104. Yet even in the worst of conditions, Frankl could still retain the last of the human freedoms, his ability to choose his attitude.

Frankl couldn't stop the guards shouting insults at him, but he could still choose whether to feel insulted. He could not help being kicked and punched by them, but he could choose to keep a dignified silence. There is internal freedom even when there is no external freedom.

How can you use your internal freedom today?

256   See the funny side

Far from living up to their reputation of being sombre killjoys, the Stoics loved humour! It is said that Chrysippus, the second head of the Stoic school, literally died in a fit of laughter.

Humour can't be an effective antidote to really serious situations, though, can it?

It can. In the concentration camps, Viktor Frankl created a special therapy for himself and a friend. Each day they invented an amusing story to tell each other about what might happen when they were liberated.

The next time you feel challenged, try finding a humorous response.

257   Consider the nature of things

'If you wish your children, and your wife, and your friends to live for ever, you are stupid; for you wish to be in control of things which you cannot.'

Epictetus, *Handbook* 14

Epictetus, as usual, tells it how he sees it. Nothing lasts for ever – not things, not people. If you expect otherwise, you are setting yourself up for unnecessary distress.

It is in this spirit that he recommends some tough premeditations of adversity. We should start off small, with something like a favourite cup, and then work our way up to people we love.

'Remind yourself when you embrace your wife or child that you embrace a mortal. Then "if either of them dies, you can bear it".'

Handbook 3

The more we appreciate the mortality of those we love, the more we appreciate them in the here and now.

258   Returning my phone

From Eric Weiner – journalist, author, recovering malcontent whose books include *The Geography of Bliss* and *The Socrates Express*

One day, my smartphone slipped from my hands, landing on the pavement HARD. A spiderweb of fissures radiated from ground zero in the upper left corner. Shards of glass protruded.

There are people who handle life's minor setbacks with aplomb, but I'm not one of them. I spent the next several hours cursing while googling 'shattered screen' on my shattered phone. I must have lost a pint of blood.

Then I paused and thought of the Stoics. They would dispense no pity. Had I practised 'premeditated adversity', I would have seen this minor catastrophe coming. Besides, while I can't undo what happened, I can control my reaction. I can assent to my 'pre-emotion' or not. I can sulk or not. It is my choice.

The Stoic teacher Epictetus thought relatively small setbacks, like my shattered smartphone, served as good practice for life's larger losses. Only in the Stoic worldview, I didn't lose my phone but rather I returned it. I should be no more traumatized than when I return a library book or check out of a hotel. Nothing is ours, not even our bodies. We always rent, never own.

I found this thought incredibly liberating. If there is nothing to lose, there is nothing to fear losing. Not even a fancy smartphone.

259   Embrace the dichotomy of value

'If you suffer pain because of some external cause,
what troubles you is not the thing but your decision about it,
and this it is in your power to wipe out at once.'

Marcus Aurelius, Meditations 8.47

Do you recall the dichotomy of value from Chapter 2? The Stoics believe that nothing external – and this includes good health as well as having plenty of money – determines how good or worthwhile our life is. What makes the difference is our character and practising the virtues.

The dichotomy of value is the Stoic's superpower. If you keep this in mind, then you don't need to 'suck it up' or keep a 'stiff upper lip' because, if you retain your good character, you are not really being harmed.

Your pain is wiped out, not suppressed.

260   The Stoic fighter-pilot

During the Vietnam War, Commander (later Vice Admiral) James Bond Stockdale was forced to eject from his burning plane into enemy territory. Stockdale immediately realized that he would be needing Epictetus, big time.

Not up to him were his circumstances, his station in life, his reputation and his physical condition. Up to him were his attitude and his actions. Stockdale recalled Epictetus's words about not getting to choose the role we play, but only how well we play it (*Handbook* 17).

He understood his role was to be the leader of the US captives and especially to avoid being used by the enemy as propaganda. Whatever else he said, he refused to say anything that could be used for these purposes. He even disfigured his face to stop them using pictures of him.

Stockdale was to spend over seven years in captivity, over half in solitary confinement and much of that in leg irons. It was not a pleasant experience. But by focusing on what he could control – his moral purpose to play his role with integrity – Stockdale won both a great personal and moral victory.

261   Stoicism at work: Shane's story

When a new managerial policy was introduced, Shane had grave misgivings about its likely impact. He researched the topic thoroughly, but this served only to deepen these doubts. He wrote up his findings and circulated them among his colleagues for them to co-sign a protest. Soon after, Shane was summoned into a meeting with management, to whom his report had been leaked. It was made crystal clear that he, his emails and activities were under scrutiny. Shane was escorted back to a corridor, presumably under the watch of the co-worker who had informed on him.

This and what followed were extremely traumatic, to the extent that his symptoms were diagnosed as post-traumatic stress disorder (PTSD).

How do you think Stoicism could help Shane?

262   How Stoicism helped Shane

Shane came through his workplace trauma through the support of his family and, of course, by drawing on Stoicism. This, in his words, is how Stoicism helped:

'The dichotomy of control helped me cope with my automatic anxiety thoughts and ruminative thinking. Epictetus's advice about monitoring our impressions helped as well. Over time, I strengthened my mental resilience by making letting go of what I could not control a practice. Then, when it came back, I let it go again. That way, I built up my "let it go" inner psychological muscle.

'And you can make it through serious attempts against your reputation, and even your job, which Stoicism also helps you to remember are not necessary to live well.'

263   The obstacle is the way

> 'Reversals have often led to greater fortune:
> many have fallen to rise higher.'
>
> Seneca, *Letters* 91.13

You may have heard the story of the Tibetan farmer who refuses to say that any apparent adversity, like his horse running away, is bad, because we simply don't know if such apparent misfortunes are bad. 'Maybe, but maybe not' – because the horse might come back with three other wild horses.

So, should we be agnostic as to whether things are as bad as they seem? Maybe.

Some have gone further, noting that misfortune can be the catalyst for positive character change.

Therapist Irvin Yalom noticed that cancer patients tend to 'trivialize the trivial'. Psychologists write about 'post-traumatic growth' where a serious difficulty can lead people to a deeper appreciation of life and relationships, undergoing positive philosophical change.

None of these recent findings would have surprised the Stoics.

As Ryan Holiday (2014), taking his cue from Marcus Aurelius, put it: 'The obstacle is the way.'

264   A mentor's journey

From Jay Adam – Mentor

Having been involved in criminal behaviour as a young man, I had certain traits hardwired into my thought process and worldview, which got me in a lot of trouble. Stoicism helped me shape my purpose and attain a clear understanding of what I can and cannot control.

I used my time in prison as an opportunity to really work on myself. With Stoicism as my foundation, I practised resisting the behaviours and thinking that led me to prison, and I became more resilient. I now mentor and work with young people to help them realize their full potential. I also provide them with Stoic principles they can apply in their day-to-day lives, so they are less likely to make the same mistakes I did.

265   A fortunate storm

Zeno, the founder of Stoicism, was at one time a well-to-do merchant from Cyprus. In around 303 BCE, aged about 30, he lost all his cargo in a shipwreck. Finding himself in Athens, Zeno wandered into a bookshop and chanced upon a book about Socrates. His interests turned from commerce to wisdom.

Later, Zeno thanked Fortune for driving him to philosophy. 'I made a prosperous voyage when I suffered a shipwreck,' he concluded.

What would be your fortunate storm?

266   My fortunate storm

From Piotr Stankiewicz – author of the *Manual of Reformed Stoicism* and a member of the Modern Stoicism team

Thinking about my Stoic beginnings always brings a smile to my face because it all started with a twist. I started studying Stoicism for good in summer 2006 when I got ... rejected by the Department of Philosophy at my university. Surely enough, I got admitted later on and went on to earn a doctorate. Yet, it had been really baffling in the beginning. I got rejected and then, during the summertime, I was basically wondering what to do with my life. You know that vibe when you are young, partying with friends constantly, drinking a lot, but deep down you have this gut sense that things are not as they should be. That was all me. I needed some guidance to put myself back on track and thus I turned to Stoicism. It clicked perfectly. And here I am 15 years later, as an author, philosopher and creator of Reformed Stoicism!

For more information about Piotr, go to https://piotrstankiewicz.pl/in-english/

267   The dog and the cart

When looking at wisdom, we explored *amor fati*, the notion that we should welcome whatever happens because the universe is good. If we think otherwise, it's just because we can't see the big picture.

Consider also the example of a dog tied to a cart. The dog can either struggle – in which case it will suffer and might even get strangled – or it can willingly accept its fate. When anything untoward happens, see yourself like the dog on the leash. You can struggle, you can begrudgingly accept it, or you can welcome it as a Stoic opportunity to practise the virtues.

268   How to die, Stoically

'Pass then through this little space of time according to nature, and end your journey contentedly, as the ripe olive falls, blessing nature who produced it, and thanking the tree on which it grew.'

Marcus Aurelius, *Meditations* 4.48

That's the attitude that I would like to adopt when it is my time to go.

But what if you depart before your time, before the olive is ripe? Were that to happen to me, I would see Ivan Noble, a BBC journalist who died of cancer aged 37, as my role model.

Noble wrote an inspiring 'Tumour Diary' for the BBC website during the two years when he was battling against cancer. He ended his journal with these words: 'If two or three people stop smoking as a result of anything I have ever written, then the one of them who would have got cancer will live and all my scribblings will have been worthwhile.' Even when facing death, there may be an opportunity to be a good role model and to contribute to the common good.

269   Good grief

Stoics don't think that we should be like statues – it is natural to grieve for those we have loved. But what if this grief does not improve with time? Such was the case with the ancient Roman Marcia, whose son had died several years earlier. Seneca came up with several arguments aimed at relieving Marcia's protracted grief.

He told her that there was a difference between natural and lingering grief. He reminded her that when she became a parent, she knew that losing her child was a possibility. He urged her to think of her other roles in life and her duties to the living.

Contemporary psychologists would probably have diagnosed Marcia with 'complicated grief'. They would appreciate Seneca's last point. Complicated grief often happens when someone has over-identified with a certain role in their life which they can no longer carry out, so it's helpful to remind them of their other potential roles.

Psychologists also suggest two other lines of argument, fully consistent with Stoicism. First, don't dwell on what happened or blame yourself. You can't control what's happened, so it's pointless to keep going over it.

Second, think about how you can honour the memory of the deceased – memorializing them by donating in their memory, for example. By doing so, as Seneca notes elsewhere:

> 'Let us see to it that the recollection of those whom
> we have lost becomes a pleasant memory to us.'

Letters 63.4

270   Meaning out of tragedy

Of all adversities, the death of one's child may be the hardest to bear. If they take their own life, it is still harder.

Charlie Waller was a talented, funny, popular young man with a good career. Yet he suffered from depression and took his own life aged 28. His grieving family wanted to do something that would mean that, in the future, young people had the opportunity for better treatment for mental health problems. The result was the foundation of the Charlie Waller Trust. It has since trained hundreds of psychologists in the UK in evidence-based therapies. Those therapists have gone on to treat thousands of patients. Charlie Waller's death, though tragic, was not for nothing.

Follow-up

- To reach the next level, embrace the dichotomy of value.
- The essential entry for this chapter is **245**: Stoic tests and opportunities.
- Work every day on minor adversities so you are well prepared for more serious difficulties.

CHAPTER 10
ON ANGER MANAGEMENT

If you are reading this book sequentially, you may well be finding that Stoicism is already helping you manage anger and frustration. When you apply the dichotomy of control, you come to accept many of the things that would otherwise lead to unnecessary frustration. The STOIC framework introduced in Chapter 3: Stoic serenity can be applied fruitfully to situations that would otherwise trigger anger.

So why a separate chapter on Stoic anger management? Simply because Stoics believe anger to be one of the biggest scourges on humanity, leading us far from rationality and good character. 'No plague has cost the human race more dear,' says Seneca in *On Anger* (1.2). To overcome this and defeat this most dangerous of adversaries, we may need to send in the Stoic cavalry.

Fortunately, help is readily available from Seneca's *On Anger*, one of the best anger management manuals ever written. According to Seneca, it's vital that we are clear that anger is an absolutely toxic and undesirable state, damaging to everyone. Epictetus and Marcus Aurelius's writings reinforce this idea. In this chapter, I'll be sharing my very favourite Stoic quotation – from Marcus – and expanding on its application to modern life.

So let us delay no further and begin the war that Stoics believe to be the worthiest of all: the war against anger …

271   Anger management check-in

Give yourself a mark for the following five statements where 0 = Disagree totally; 1 = Slightly disagree; 2 = Neutral or not sure; 3 = Mainly agree and 4 = Completely agree.

1. Those who know me best would say I never get angry.

2. I never get angry when driving or using public transport.

3. I'm good at noticing when I start to get irritated, and try to calm down.

4. I try to see others' points of view, even when we disagree.

5. Getting angry does more harm than good.

Now add up your total score. The *higher* your score, the more Stoic you are.

   0–6 You've come to the right chapter! Retake the test at the end of the chapter and see how much your score has improved.

   7–13 You aren't Caligula, but there's still room for improvement!

   14–20 Well done! Is your name Lucius Seneca by any chance?

272 The magic button

'My wife should be here, not me!'

It was not the most promising start to my first counselling session with Luke. He had shown up only because his wife had threatened to leave him if he didn't. It's best to avoid arguments with clients, especially ones with 'severe anger management issues', as was written on Luke's referral form.

I aimed for diplomacy. 'That may well be the case. But since you're here, how can these sessions help you?'

'You tell me. You're the counsellor,' Luke answered, testily.

'It is true that you get angry?'

'I'm not a Zen monk. But who is?'

'What I'm wondering is whether getting angry actually works for you. What do you think?'

'I'm not sure what you mean.'

'Well, if you could press a magic button that would ensure you never got angry again, ever, would you press it?'

Do the negative and stressful effects of anger have you wishing you had a magic button?

273 The case for anger

Luke didn't want to change, because he felt justified in his anger. 'Anger means people don't take advantage of me,' he said. 'When I walk in the room, my kids stop what they are doing and look up at me. Anger helps me win people's respect.'

Not for the first time, I wished that Seneca was with me in the counselling room to help me out. He would have told Luke about Caligula, the despotic emperor who thought that everyone respected him when they actually feared and hated him. Caligula mistook fear for respect. My hunch was that the same was true of Luke. How could I get him to see this? Perhaps he had experienced his own personal Caligula.

'Let's turn the tables,' I said, eager to shift Luke's perspective. 'Can you remember any time that you've stopped what you were doing when someone walked in the room?'

Luke thought for a moment, then replied, 'Sure. My dad, after he'd been drinking.'

'Nice guy?'

'No, he was a right b*****d.'

'Do you want to be like your dad?'

'That's the last thing I want.'

And just like that, the argument for anger was dismissed.

274 · A temporary madness

When we get angry, the red mist descends and we quite literally lose our minds.

In *On Anger*, Seneca tells the story of Vedius Pollo, who thought his banquet had been ruined when a clumsy slave broke a glass. Furious, Vedius ordered the poor wretch to be thrown as food into a pool of lampreys (3.40), although he was saved by the intervention of the emperor Augustus.

No wonder Seneca thought of anger as temporary madness. Anger is, he says,

> 'equally devoid of self-control, regardless of decorum,
> forgetful of kinship, obstinately engrossed in whatever
> it begins to do, deaf to reason and advice, excited by trifling
> causes, awkward at perceiving what is true and just.'

On Anger 1.1

That was certainly true of Vedius Pollo, but how about you?

Have you nearly done something in a fit of anger that you wouldn't be able to undo?

275   The worst thing about anger

Have you ever seen what you look like when you get angry?

Seneca recommends that angry people look at themselves in the mirror – hands trembling, body swaying, veins swollen (*On Anger* 2.35). Is this the look you want to be known for?

But that's not the worst thing about anger. Anger causes high blood pressure and increased risk of heart attacks, strokes and other serious health problems. Even worse, it takes away our most precious commodity: our ability to think rationally and to act with justice.

That's the very worst thing about anger.

276 'The sword of justice is ill-placed in the hands of an angry person' (Seneca, *On Anger* 1.19)

Imagine that you are in the dock, accused of a crime you didn't commit. What sort of doubts would you want the jury to raise before they convicted you? Maybe you'd like them to ask questions like these:

- How strong is the evidence against you?
- Was the crime intentional?
- Are there any mitigating circumstances?
- Even if you are guilty, should you really be held prisoner?

Now think back to the last time you got angry at someone and switch roles with them. Did you ask any of these questions, giving them the benefit of the doubt? Or was your mindset more like that of a kangaroo court, presuming guilt and thirsting for revenge?

Seneca was dead right. The sword of justice is indeed ill-placed in the hands of an angry person.

277 Dutch courage

Some people say that anger gives them courage. But have you heard the expression 'Dutch courage'? It's the false confidence you get from drinking alcohol … like the confidence of an embarrassing uncle at a wedding, dancing wildly after a few drinks.

Like alcohol, anger spurs you to action, but you are likely to regret it the next morning!

We need to foster courage infused with wisdom, not the fake bravado that accompanies anger.

278   Don't give them the power

Early in my career, I remember one client who began plotting revenge against her ex. 'I know someone I can get to torch his car,' she enjoyed telling me. Horrified, I tried my best to get her to reflect on the possible consequences of such action – without much apparent impact.

At our next meeting, I nervously inquired about her plot.

'Oh that! A friend advised me not to stoop to his level. I'm not going to give him that kind of power over me!'

Her friend had been a much more effective counsellor than me!

Maybe they had read Marcus Aurelius's suggestion that the best revenge is to be unlike your enemy (*Meditations* 6.6). Or perhaps, as the Stoics think, wisdom is available to anyone who reflects on life and its lessons.

279   Life's too short

If you had only one day to live, how much of that day would you spend being angry? Seneca expresses this insight more powerfully.

'Why should we, as though we were born to live for ever, waste our tiny span of life in declaring anger against anyone? Why should days, which we might spend in honourable enjoyment, be misapplied in grieving and torturing others? Life is a matter which does not admit of waste, and we have no spare time to throw away.'

On Anger 3.42

How much time has anger stolen from you?

280   The home that anger built ...

Another client, Christine, was so polite and friendly that I could hardly believe she had a problem with anger management. Her eyes welled up with tears as she admitted that she frequently 'lost the plot' with her young children, shouting at them when they were late for school or bickering in the car.

I thought that Seneca's ideas on anger might help, and so I gave them to her as homework. She loved Seneca!

> 'Anger is very like a falling rock which breaks itself to pieces upon the very thing which it crushes.'
>
> *On Anger* 1.1

This quotation spoke to her especially, and she set it as her home screen.

Is anger breaking you, and breaking into your home?

281   Moderate anger?

James was initially sceptical about the Stoic arguments against anger:

'What the Stoics are arguing against isn't anger, it's rage. Surely *moderate* anger is OK? Wasn't it Aristotle who said that anger can be appropriate, as long as we're angry with the right person, to the right degree and at the right time?'

'So,' I replied, 'you think that moderate anger is a feasible option. The Stoics disagree. Would you be interested in doing an experiment to see who has got it right?'

I asked James to keep a log of all the times he got angry, and whether he was able to employ moderate anger – or not ...

This is the information I asked him to log:

Situation	Actions	Consequences
What triggered my anger?	What did I do?	Was it beneficial?

Today's challenge is to keep this log yourself.

Find out for yourself whether moderate anger is, as the Stoics believe, a pipe dream.

282   An experiment in anger

Next session, James sheepishly entered the counselling room.

'I took my wife out to dinner the day after our session. We both ordered smoked salmon – hardly complicated – as our starter. We waited ages, and diners who arrived after us got their food first. I was seething, but then I remembered to try to *moderate* anger – defusing the situation with a joke. "What's the delay?" I asked the waitress. "Are you catching the salmon yourself?"

'They took something off the bill, but it took the gloss off the evening. Worse, my wife complained that I was being a bit of a dick. Maybe it's time to try a more Stoic approach …'

283   Reasons to obliterate anger

Here's a handy list of all the reasons Stoics give for not getting angry:

■ Anger harms those you love as well as yourself.

■ Moderate anger is not a realistic option.

■ Life is too short to waste it getting angry.

■ The word of justice is ill-placed in the hands of the angry person.

■ Anger is like Dutch courage.

- Anger is a temporary madness.
- Anger does terrible things to our bodies – and, worse, to our minds.
- When you get angry you're descending to the other person's level.
- Angry people don't get respect – they're feared and hated.

Which of these reasons resonates most with you?

284 Exercising a zero-tolerance policy to anger

Suppose you've decided that the Stoics are right. The question then becomes how you can best control anger.

This was the position of Christine, the young mother struggling with her children:

'I want to practise a zero-tolerance policy not towards my children's behaviour but towards my own anger. But I need help!'

I suggested that she keep a log of situations in which she got angry in this format:

Situation	First signs of anger	Angry thoughts
What triggered my anger?	What were the first signs I was getting angry or frustrated?	What thoughts drove my anger? In particular, were there any 'shoulds' or 'musts' or ideas about fairness?

Keep this log yourself, today.

285   Catch your anger early

'The best plan is to reject straightaway the first incentives to anger, to resist its very beginnings, and to take care not to be betrayed into it: for if once it begins to carry us away, it is hard to get back again into a healthy condition.'

Seneca, *On Anger* 1.8

Seneca advises us to catch our anger early – before it gets a head of steam. We can do this by noticing:

■ the type of situations which trigger anger

■ what happens biologically when we get angry

■ the thoughts that work us into an angry state.

That's why I had asked Christine to keep a log. She came back with this entry:

Situation	First signs of anger	Angry thoughts
School run	Clenched fists	This is going to be another stressful morning. I don't deserve this.
Elder child looking for school kit when it's already late		He should have got this already last night. Why can't he be more responsible?

Christine detected some clear patterns. She got angry mainly on the school run. Her mind was full of thoughts about the 'shoulds', 'musts' and fairness as she clenched the steering wheel.

What are the tell-tale signs that you are about to lose the plot?

286   The three phases of anger

Seneca's theory about the three phases of anger is of great practical help in anger management.

Phase 1: Anger is triggered and our body sets itself up to attack. This is the automatic fight/flight response.

Phase 2: An instant later, our rational brain attempts to interpose. This is our window of opportunity to evaluate the situation rationally – or not!

Phase 3: The end result. Worst-case scenario is when we have exacerbated the fight/flight with angry thoughts. We're seeing red and are beyond reason. Seneca likens the angry person to someone who has fallen off the edge of a precipice – they are past the point of no return.

Does Seneca's theory sound familiar?

287   Fawlty anger management

Did you ever watch that great British sitcom *Fawlty Towers*? One of my favourite episodes is when Basil Fawlty, the irascible hotelier, winds up angrily beating his broken-down car with a branch. *Sheer madness!* Type 'Basil attacks his car' into your search engine to find the video clip. It's very funny and a great illustration of what Seneca and the Stoics are talking about.

Basil is in a hurry and when his car won't start, he panics. This is Phase 1 of anger.

A Stoic would take a step back and make a rational plan about how to deal with the situation, but not Basil. He adds fuel to the flames by thinking the car has it in for him and is purposely treating him unfairly.

The result? Basil falls off the edge of the precipice of rationality, talking to his car and thrashing it with a branch.

As Seneca said, anger is a temporary madness ...

288   When can we control anger?

Anger can be controlled; it's all a matter of good timing.

There is no point trying to suppress the automatic fight/flight reaction, though you *can* soothe it (by taking some deep breaths for instance).

If you only catch anger at Phase 3, however, it's too late to do much. You can perform damage control by leaving the situation, though.

Here is where most of our control lies:

- *Before* you get angry, arming yourself with a good strategy to deal with likely provocations.
- Or *after* the fight/flight reaction – Seneca's Phase 2 – when we can marshal our rationality and work out how to deal with the situation virtuously.

Wise anger management means exercising control at the right time.

289   It's your call

Before we get irate, there is always a choice about how to respond. We can either choose to press the gas pedal when we buy into angry thoughts like 'It's not fair' or 'I need to teach them a lesson'. Or we can remind ourselves that what other people do isn't under our control and anger never helps. We can also be mindful of when we're catastrophizing.

To be or not to be uselessly irate.

It's your call.

290   Plead the case for the defence, not the prosecution

Christine, the stressed-out mum, laughed when I showed her the Basil Fawlty clip to illustrate faulty anger management. She resonated with Basil's taking on the role of the victim and then acting like a prosecutor: 'I do that all the time with my kids.'

She was completely up for trying to plead the case for the *defence* instead of the *prosecution*.

I showed her the questions we saw in 276: 'The sword of justice is ill-placed in the hands of an angry person.' Christine adapted them to create her own plea for the targets of her anger.

Do the kids mean any harm? *No, they're just being kids.*

Are they doing anything that bad? *No, they're just being kids …*

Is getting angry going to help? *Clearly, it hasn't worked so far!*

Christine took this list away and read it each morning as she made the kids' breakfast. This helped her have it in mind during the school run. She reported managing her anger '100 per cent better'.

Could coming up with such a list of questions and rational responses help you manage your anger better?

291   What virtues do I need?

Christine was no longer getting angry with her kids, but she still was not entirely happy. Her kids were still slow-moving in the morning, sometimes arriving late for school. Clearly, shouting at everyone wasn't the answer – but something needed to be done.

Once again, Stoicism has the answer.

I introduced Christine to the four cardinal virtues and asked her which ones might be useful.

Self-control – *I think I've learned that now, thank you.*

Justice – *I've been doing that when I've been making the case for the defence, haven't I?*

Courage – *Well, it's pretty courageous me coming here and owning up to my problem.*

Wisdom – *Hmmm … That's what I'm lacking, a wise solution to the problem of my kids running late.*

What advice would you give Christine?

292　Don't get mad, get virtuous!

Christine decided to take a parenting skills course which armed her with a whole battery of useful skills. She decided to train her children to prepare everything they needed for school the night before.

Additionally, she began to enforce consequences on her children if they bickered – such as pulling over the car until they stopped arguing, even if that meant they would be late for school. She learned about *assertiveness* – that blend of courage to express your needs and the wisdom to know how to do this in a non-threatening and calm manner.

After a few more sessions, Christine reported that her children's behaviour had improved as much as her anger management.

What virtues do you need as an alternative to getting mad?

293   My favourite Stoic passage –
         Meditations 2.1

My favourite Stoic passage also happens to be very relevant to anger management. It is rather famous and worth quoting in full:

'Begin the morning by saying to yourself, I shall meet with the busybody, the ungrateful, arrogant, deceitful, envious, unsocial. All these things happen to them by reason of their ignorance of what is good and evil. But I who have seen the nature of the good that it is beautiful … I can neither be injured by any of them, for no one can fix on me what is ugly, nor can I be angry with my kinsman, nor hate him. For we are made for co-operation, like feet, like hands, like eyelids, like the rows of the upper and lower teeth. To act against one another then is contrary to nature; and it is acting against one another to be vexed and to turn away.'

Marcus Aurelius, *Meditations* 2.1

We don't know whether Marcus Aurelius had a problem with anger management, but I am sure that, if he had, reading this every morning would have helped him enormously!

Read it a few times. What Stoic wisdom do you take from *Meditations* 2.1?

294   How *Meditations* 2.1 can help you
         manage anger and frustration

Personally, I take these four big messages from *Meditations* 2.1:

1. Being prepared for people to be annoying can help you deal with it.

2. Don't assume people do wrong intentionally. In their minds, they think they're behaving rightly.

3. It's wrong to turn away from other people because we are made to work together and co-operate. Forgive and turn towards them.

4. Other people can't really harm you anyway. They can't prevent you being virtuous or performing your roles well, and that's what's most important.

295   Premeditation of anger

My own anger triggers include cold calls from insurance companies. It's proved helpful to rehearse this trigger and how to handle it.

Like Marcus in *Meditations* 2.1, I remind myself that these people aren't trying to be irritating, they are just doing their job. All their call is costing me is a bit of time, and it's time well spent if I use it to build my character.

It so happened that I had to deal with an insurance company while writing this chapter. Before the call, I imagined the agent sitting in their home having to make this scripted call over and over, every day, just to pay their bills. So, I rehearsed being pleasant to them.

I was very friendly and calm when we spoke. In fact, the agent turned out to be super helpful.

Try the premeditation of anger to make the everyday unpleasantries more pleasant.

296   It's not their fault

Carmelo Di Maria – the founder of London Stoics – found himself very frustrated with his father's foreign live-in carer. He couldn't understand her, although he did get the impression she supported some politicians he found repulsive! When he asked her to repeat what she said, she got het up as if he was the source of the problem. How do you think a good Stoic would approach this? Answer it yourself, before reading Carmelo's answer.

'Luckily enough, I had my Stoic journal with me. So, I jotted down what the situation was, what my feelings were, and how to best frame the issue to gain some equanimity and peace of mind. I said to myself that it wasn't her fault if she still hadn't mastered the language and that it was a good opportunity for me to practise patience and understanding. Every morning, I would also practise a Stoic morning meditation, i.e. preparing myself for the day ahead, knowing I would have to face her and that I would have to keep my calm. Lesson learned? That you need to try to tune in to other people's difficulties and challenges.'

297   The power of forgiveness

From Ranjini George – author of *Through My Mother's Window: Emirati Women Tell Their Stories and Recipes*

It is the day after Mother's Day and I wake up sad and angry. Why didn't my husband celebrate me? Ah, I am not the mother of his sons. The roses were perfunctory. Last night, I walked my Shih Tzu on empty streets in suburban Mississauga. I imagined happy mothers beaming over their celebratory dinners.

I read a quotation from my calendar, where the Dalai Lama reminds us that we take back control through forgiveness.

I read Marcus: 'When the force of circumstances causes you, in some sense, to lose your equilibrium, return to yourself with all speed ... for you will be more in control of the measure if you return to it again and again.' I wake up to the opportunity to practise: yes, forgiveness – to drop the notion, 'I have been harmed.'

I question my attachment to the customary tokens of Mother's Day celebrations.

Aren't these celebrations geared towards consumerism rather than genuine love? My beloved husband celebrates me in his open-hearted patient listening and in the space that he allows me to grow. One day does not cancel a thousand, ten thousand: the honey-dense life my husband and I share.

You can read more of Ranjini's work at https://ranjinigeorge.wordpress.com/

298   The real meaning of Father's Day

It was Father's Day and only one card had arrived from my children (both away at university). I was beginning to feel a bit miffed. After all I had done for them, and they couldn't even remember a card!

Before the irritation grew into something worse, *Meditations* 2.1 came to my rescue. I reminded myself that this was merely forgetfulness, nothing worse. To feel angry, and turn away from them, would be contrary to nature.

I recalled Epictetus's advice to think about what you do to other people rather than what they do to you (*Handbook* 30). Had I got it the wrong way round? Should Father's Day be less about me being pampered and more about my stepping up to be a good father?

By the time my children called, Marcus and Epictetus had melted away my childish self-centredness. I turned the conversation around to my kids' concerns, gladly offering practical assistance where I could. It turned out that a parcel (no mere card) was on its way from child 2!

Next year, I will try to remember the real meaning of Father's Day.

299   Vicious and virtuous cycles

From Peter Cooper – author of *Escape to Budapest*

After taking a month-long course on Modern Stoicism, I found that my general state of happiness had increased, and this continued as my Stoic habits became embedded.

Previously, I had become too reactive to relatively trivial events, especially those relating to some annoying neighbours. My Stoicism helped me understand that I could not control them. I could, however, control my reaction to them. By taking a step back, my anger management became much better.

Avoiding such instant negative thinking seemed to compound the space it left for positive thoughts. But it was better than that. For a good Stoic does not just avoid difficult events, they consider what they can learn from them and innovate ways to tackle the issue.

If you are an angry person, you never get this far, but remain locked in a vicious cycle of negative feedback. Stoicism helped me turn this cycle of negativity and anger into a virtuous cycle of positivity and calm assertiveness.

300 WAR: the three steps needed to win the good war against anger

Now you realize how to win the war against anger. From here it's just a case of remembering these ideas and putting them into practice. As it happens, 'WAR' is an acronym for the three steps you need to beat anger.

W stands for *Why* – all the reasons the Stoics give for obliterating anger (**272–83**).

A is for *Awareness*. Become aware of the patterns of your own anger, aiming to control it at the right time (**284–9**).

R stands for *Rational response*. Stoicism does *not* propose that you roll over in the face of injustices. Instead, think about the situation rationally and apply the appropriate virtues.

Follow-up

■ Retake the self-assessment in **271** and compare your results.

■ The essential entry in this chapter is **300**: WAR: the three steps needed to win the good war against anger.

■ Follow Epictetus and keep a tally of how many days you go without getting worked up.

CHAPTER 11
THE SHORTNESS OF LIFE

Time is our greatest gift, yet it is one that we are all too prone to fritter away.

To manage time well, argue the Stoics, we must first come to terms with death.

Although it may seem a bitter pill, awareness of our own mortality is the most powerful medicine the Stoics offer against complacency. They offer us two related techniques you will learn about in this chapter – the premeditation of our own death (*premeditatio malorum*) and deliberate reminders of death (*memento mori*).

Death itself is not so terrible, it is wasting life that is the problem. Seneca offers many practical tools to help you manage time better. In fact, his classic essay *On the Shortness of Life* reads much like a modern, and particularly astute, time management manual.

You may feel like skipping over some of the entries in this chapter. If you are recently bereaved or otherwise feeling vulnerable, that may be prudent. But for most of us, learning how to manage time well is a good investment. We cannot control how long we exist on this planet, but we can control whether we spend that time well.

The gift of the message of *On the Shortness of Life*, written to Seneca's father-in-law, never stops giving.

301   Nothing to fear in death

> 'I can't escape death, but can't I escape the dread of it?'
>
> Epictetus, *Discourses* 1.27

In his *Handbook*, Epictetus says that we shouldn't fear death, since Socrates did not think that death was dreadful. Playing devil's advocate, I would ask Epictetus, 'Why should I trust Socrates? He believed in an afterlife. What if I don't?'

But Socrates has this possibility covered. If there isn't an afterlife, says Socrates, being dead is like being in a dreamless sleep. And what is so dreadful about that?

302   Life and death parallel

What do you feel about all the time that existed before you were born?

Right. You weren't there to feel anything.

So why feel any different about the time after you die? You won't be there, you won't feel anything.

Being dead is not agonizing. Realizing all the time you *could* have spent doing things meaningful and worthwhile is.

Make the most of your time on Earth and death is nothing to fear.

303   Death is natural

Marcus Aurelius emphasizes another reason not to fear death: it's natural.

> 'It's natural. And nothing natural is evil.'
> Marcus Aurelius, *Meditations* 2.17

A rose blooms and then wilts and dies. In the same way we are born, live and then die. We are dissolved back into the elements from which we came – reunited with nature.

Do not think that you have lost someone, but rather they have returned to nature.

304   Quality not quantity

A key Stoic idea is that it is the quality of life that is important, more than the quantity.

A good friend of mine was diagnosed with a terminal illness in his forties. He was able to face his death with equanimity. 'I've had a good life,' he told me, a few weeks before he died.

An unhappy, bad life would not be any better for being long. A life can be happy and good even if relatively short.

305   Avoidance backfires

I am afraid that my mother, were she still alive, would have skipped those last four entries. She was so worried about cancer that she banned anyone in her earshot from mentioning the word. But this meant that death for her was always a bogeyman, lurking in the shadows.

Avoidance often backfires, making us psychologically inflexible and finding the very thing we fear showing up everywhere.

The famous writer Fyodor Dostoevsky discovered this for himself:

'Try to pose for yourself this task: not to think of a polar bear, and you will see that the cursed thing will come to mind every minute.'
An Essay Concerning the Bourgeois, p. 49

Daniel Wegner, a Harvard psychology professor, wrote a whole book about the problem – *White Bears and Other Unwanted Thoughts*. The unwanted thoughts include, of course, thoughts about dying.

Try not to think about death and, paradoxically, you just give death more force.

306   No laughing matter?

A gentle way to think about death is to list all the euphemisms we have for it. How many can you think of?

It may not be a coincidence that one of the funniest sketches contains *a lot* of euphemisms for death. Today's Stoic challenge is to watch (or re-watch) Monty Python's 'Dead Parrot Sketch'.

In it, the John Cleese character returns to a pet store with the parrot he purchased there – it's not that the parrot is slightly defective, it's completely bereft of life; it's a stiff, it's stone dead. To drive the point home that the parrot is DEAD, he lists still more ways to describe its lifeless state – 'gone to meet 'is maker!', 'shuffled off 'is mortal coil!' and 11 other hilarious ways to describe death.

The parrot falling off its perch when the cage was shaken was certainly a dead giveaway. Looking on the bright side of life, the shopkeeper does agree to exchange it in the end …

Death is inescapable and a fate we all have in common. It's OK to laugh about it.

307 How not to waste your life

'The life we receive is not short, but we make it so.'

Seneca, *On the Shortness of Life* 1.4

Could this be true for you? Today, keep a diary to find out.

I suggest using this format. The third column is your estimate of how well you used your time.

Time	Activity	Mark/10	Insight

There are 692,040 hours in the average lifespan. How well did you spend this last 24?

308   Your time will tell

'People closely guard their money, but when it comes
to wasting time, which they should be most careful
about, they are the most prodigal.'

Seneca, *On the Shortness of Life* 3

Jo found tracking her time to be *really* helpful. Here are entries she found especially enlightening.

Time	Activity	Mark/10	Insight
7–8am	Had breakfast, got up, read newspapers, looked at Facebook.	5/10	I spent too long cruising through celebrity clickbait articles!
11–12am	In a long meeting that could have been summed up in an email.	1/10	This was a waste of time!
8–9pm	Went out with old friends I hadn't seen for ages. Enjoyable and reminded me of the value of friendship.	9/10	This genuinely felt like time well spent.

Jo's diary informs her that she spends too much time reading gossip rags and not enough time with those she loves. She decides to:

■ trade morning scrolling for gratitude journaling, starting the day on a peaceful note

■ make a strong case for opting out of one specific weekly work meeting

■ schedule to see one of her best friends whom she hasn't seen for a while.

Clickbait will be here until the end of time; our loved ones won't.

Where can your time be better spent?

309   Never short of time? Pull the other one ...

> 'Let us balance life's books each day. One who daily
> puts the finishing touches to their life is never short of time.'
>
> Seneca, *Letters* 101

Jennifer begs to differ. 'Never short of time? Pull the other one ...' A single mum, Jennifer must feed the kids, take them to school, clean up and then go to work. Jennifer nevertheless completes her time management diary. She learns that Seneca is right.

These are her two key insights:

1. Before she leaves for work, she tidies up the house as if visitors were expected.

2. At work, she often volunteers to do what isn't mandatory. She almost never asks for help, and even takes work home on weekends.

Jennifer resolves to spend 15 minutes less tidying up each day. She also creates a healthy boundary between her home and work lives and practises saying no.

Her days cannot go on being an uphill battle. She recalls Marcus Aurelius – of course an injured soldier should ask for help if they need it (*Meditations* 7.7). So, she's decided to also practise asking for help.

Are you spending too much time adding unnecessary stress?

310   Swallowed

'Those vices of yours will swallow up your time.'

Seneca, *On the Shortness of Life* 6

Sally spends hours deciding what to buy online – and then more time returning items she doesn't want.

Seema puts off doing her college work to binge-watch *Peaky Blinders*.

Jack gets into arguments with his partner because she says he doesn't do his share of the housework.

As Seneca points out, vices swallow up our time. What vices swallow up time for Sally, Seema and Jack?

311   Save time! Choose virtue!

An unlikely advertising slogan perhaps, but, according to the Stoics, a very helpful one. Here are my suggestions about how Sally, Seema and Jack can save time:

■ Sally requires self-control to do less online shopping.

■ Seema requires courage to overcome her fear of discomfort.

■ Jack needs more justice to do his share of the housework.

They all need wisdom, to understand that this is the virtue they need, and to know how to apply it.

What virtues can you call on to save your valuable time?

312   Stop people-pleasing

> 'The condition of all who are preoccupied is wretched,
> but most wretched is the condition of those who labour
> at preoccupations that are not even their own.'
>
> Seneca, *On the Shortness of Life* 1.19

This is your life. But how much time do you spend working towards other people's agendas rather than your own? Seneca is not suggesting you stop being compassionate or fair; he is not suggesting that you become selfish. He is talking about our tendency to care too much what other people think.

Today, pay attention to your motivation. Whenever you notice yourself doing things purely to please others or because you think that they might judge you, remember – this is your life; don't give other people that much power.

313   Stoicism for procrastinators

> 'Do not wander from your path any longer ... Hasten to the
> goal ... if you care at all for yourself, while still you may.'
>
> Marcus Aurelius, *Meditations* 3.14

Procrastination is one of the most common issues presented in short-term therapy. I guess it would be the clear winner if the worst procrastinators ever got round to booking a session ... Yes, it's easy to laugh at procrastination, but it can have a serious impact on well-being.

Can Stoicism help? Absolutely. Here are my top three Stoic tips for procrastinators:

1. Forget about trying to make things perfect. You can't control whether they are perfect – that's largely down to other people's perceptions, which you can't control. Aim instead at doing something that is good enough.

2. Focus on your goal rather than how you feel. Remember, too, that those feelings may not be a trustworthy guide. The task you are avoiding is nearly always something that makes you uncomfortable, like writing that assignment or doing that spring clean. Remind yourself that you can cope with the discomfort; it's just a dispreferred indifferent.

3. Use your virtues. Have the self-control to avoid displacement activities, the wisdom to break tasks down into tiny steps, and the courage to take that first step.

What are *you* avoiding? Use these tips to make a start today.

314   Busy doing nothing

> 'It would be tedious to mention all the different men who have spent the whole of their life over chess or ball or the practice of baking their bodies in the sun.'
>
> Seneca, *On the Shortness of Life* 13

What would you want written on your gravestone? That you spent your life sunbathing? That you played games?

Such activities might be OK in small doses but should be considered recreation, which there is a time and place for. Seneca's point is that we are made for greater things.

If Seneca knew what you did yesterday, what would he have said about the way you spent your leisure time?

315   What about 'flow'?

Seneca has a special word for those he thinks are engaged in 'busy idleness' which is usually translated as 'the engrossed' or 'the preoccupied'.

Flow is an idea popularized by psychologist Mihaly Csikszentmihalyi. You are in flow when you are totally absorbed in what you are doing – like a tennis player being 'in the zone' or two friends immersed in conversation. A great example of a man in flow is Martin Luther King during his 1963 'I Have a Dream' speech.

If flow is in the service of something good – as in King's speech – then it is good. However, flow can often be addictive. A teenager hooked on video games, for example, or the husband who deserts his family duties to play golf. Myself, I have to guard against playing virtual bridge too much!

Where in your life do you experience 'good flow' – being absorbed in things that are truly worthwhile?

Where do you experience 'bad flow' – being immersed in things that looking at the big picture of your life, aren't such a good use of your time?

316   Stoicism during a pandemic

From Brittany Polat – co-founder of Stoicare and part of the Modern Stoicism and Stoic Fellowship teams

It's always great to be a Stoic, but never more so than during a global health crisis. When the pandemic struck in 2020, Stoicism helped me deal with the reality of staying at home with my three young children while also home-schooling them and working remotely. A few months later, when my whole family came down with the virus, Stoicism helped me care for everyone on my own (no one else could be near us) while also being sick myself.

Perhaps more than anything else, Stoicism helped me win the mental game against fear and panic that so often accompanied COVID-19. Through my practice of *premeditatio malorum* and *memento mori*,

I was prepared for hardship, sickness and even potential death. The realization that life is fleeting and precious allowed us to enjoy our time together, even under trying circumstances.

317 *Memento mori*

> 'Do not act as if you were going to live ten thousand years.
> Death hangs over you.'
>
> Marcus Aurelius, *Meditations* 4.17

If you were going to live a thousand years, then frittering away a few decades wouldn't matter nearly so much. Thinking about death makes us uncomfortable, but this cost is outweighed by being a remedy for complacency.

Memento mori – reminders that we must die – can help. For example:

- a skull
- wilted flowers
- a picture of a much younger you
- a cemetery visit.

The list is not exhaustive; you might have an idea that works better for you. Today's challenge is to experiment with various *memento mori* and find out which works best for you.

Please note: If you're suffering a recent bereavement, this might be one experiment to skip.

318 Dead poets' wisdom

> 'Hasten to live and imagine each day as a separate life.'
>
> Seneca, *Letters* 101.10

My personal favourite *memento mori* is a scene in *Dead Poets Society*. The charismatic English teacher Mr Keating (played by Robin Williams) shows his new class a group photograph of students from long ago. They were once young and full of dreams, but now they're dead … Every one of them, fertilizing daffodils, their dreams gone largely unfulfilled.

Mr Keating addresses the class as if there was nothing more important than to remember the shortness of life: 'If you listen real close … you can hear them whisper … Seize the day, boys. Make your lives extraordinary.'

The Latin phrase for 'seize the day' is *carpe diem*.

How will you seize the day?

319   Live each day as if it was your last

> 'Perfection of character possesses this: to live each day
> as if the last, to be neither feverish nor apathetic,
> and not to act a part.'
>
> Marcus Aurelius, *Meditations* 7.69

For the Stoic, living each day as if it was your last does not mean going on a hedonistic frenzy because there are no consequences. Quite the reverse.

It means striving to be the person you want to be *today*, not tomorrow.

Today, imagine it might be your last, and bring urgency to the task of perfecting your character.

We are not promised a tomorrow … Be the best version of yourself today.

320   Cemetery run

From Scott Perry – Chief Difference-Maker at Creative on Purpose

My wife and I sold the farm where we raised fruit, vegetables, chickens, pets, our two sons, and more than a few eyebrows. Days later, I came within a few inches of being hit by a car on my daily run to the cemetery and back.

The irony was obvious. Just a few days after we'd sold it, I nearly 'bought the farm'.

What to do?

To avoid ending up in the graveyard, I now drive there to get my daily exercise. The cemetery is located at the highest point in town. The Blue Ridge Mountains are visible in the distance. The acreage is beautifully landscaped. Beyond the tombstones lie fields and farms.

Being surrounded by the beauty of nature and reminders of my mortality helps me embrace the ancient practice of *memento mori*: 'Remember, you die.'

Embracing life's impermanence cultivates acceptance and equanimity. While engaged in the difficult work of making a difference, I'm also in pursuit of living well.

Life is a gift. It doesn't matter where you believe it comes from. Accepting this acknowledges that it is both yours and not yours.

Contemplating your death is to consider what it means to be human and genuinely happy – and a call to action to strive for both.

You and I can't know how long we keep this gift. It is that uncertainty that allows us to make meaning and find the motivation to live well – and live for others – while we can.

What's death for?

That it ends is at the heart of life's value. The worth of your life is measured by your contributions. The quality of your contributions is determined by your character and extent of your effort.

Legacy isn't the monuments and money you leave behind. Legacy is the difference you're making today.

Meditate on your death. Then take whatever you have left and live it on purpose.

321   Premeditation of the ultimate adversity

Premeditation of adversity is a key Stoic practice. Are you ready for a piece of shock therapy, the ultimate adversity premeditation?

Imagine that you're out of time. No details needed; you've died.

Spend a few moments noticing your feelings and thoughts about this. I recommend setting a timer for three minutes. What are your main regrets? What do you wish you had done differently? Then open your eyes and write down what came up.

Then make a resolution to do *one thing differently* today as a result.

322   Shock therapy

Robbie, a 45-year-old married man with two children, found the premeditation of death to be very effective. This is what he wrote down:

> 'I felt very sad. Why haven't I told my wife and kids how much I love them? Why haven't I taken better care of my health? Why haven't I used my whole life better? Why haven't I made up with a few people I fell out with?

'What am I going to do differently today?

'I should tell everyone how much I care for them. I can do that.

'I am also going to text my old mate Max, who I kind of fell out with over nothing a year or two back. I'll suggest we bury the hatchet, and not in each other!

'Wow – I didn't know that exercise was going to be quite so powerful!'

323   A Stoic lifeline

This Stoic lifeline exercise is another powerful exercise that combines elements of both *memento mori* and the premeditation of adversity.

Imagine that the line below represents your life:

————————————————X————————————————

One end represents your birth and the other your death. The big X represents where you are now.

1. Spend a minute meditating on the line and where you are now (the X).

2. Next, reflect on some things that you would like to do before you die. This is your *conventional* bucket list.

3. Next, reflect on how you would like to change the world for the better. Then think on the necessary qualities needed to become a person who makes positive change. This is your *Stoic* bucket list.

4. Write down your two bucket lists in the spaces below.

My conventional bucket list

(*things I want to do*)

My Stoic bucket list

(*the differences I want to make in the world; the qualities I want to develop*)

5. Finally, reflect on how doing this exercise could make a positive difference to your life and jot down your answer to that.

324   A Stoic bucket list

Sally might be thought to be young, at 28, to be doing her bucket list, but she found the Stoic version of the exercise very interesting. This is what she came up with:

My conventional bucket list

(*things I want to do*)

Get married

Have kids

Travel the world

Run a half-marathon

Goodness, I am quite conventional, aren't I?!

My Stoic bucket list

(*the differences I want to make in the world; the qualities I want to develop*)

I want to work on my courage — the only thing I have to fear is fear itself!

I would also like to work on wisdom — learning about Stoicism is a great step.

Although I may not make ground-breaking discoveries that have a profound impact, I do want to make a difference in the lives of those I encounter each day, especially my family.

How this answer can make a positive difference:

I felt more enlightened by the Stoic list. It revealed what I need to do to fulfil what's listed on my conventional bucket list. Courage can help me run the half-marathon — and find a good life partner! I realize I'm a positive force in the world simply by making a difference in the lives of those around me. That's under my control, and I find that idea rather inspiring.

325 Don't act as if you are going to live for a thousand years

St Augustine (not a Stoic) is famously paraphrased as saying: 'Please God, make me good, but not just yet.'

Marcus Aurelius thought otherwise:

> 'While you live, while you may, become good.'
>
> *Meditations* 4.17

And Seneca agreed with Marcus:

> 'What foolish forgetfulness of mortality to postpone good plans.'
>
> *On the Shortness of Life* 3

What are *you* putting off?

326 Six months to live

> 'Undertake each action as one aware they may next moment depart out of life.'
>
> Marcus Aurelius, *Meditations* 2.11

Another exercise that my students and clients have found helpful is to answer this question:

How would you spend your time if you only had six healthy months to live? What would you do more? What would you do less?

Then reflect on this:

How can your answers to these questions positively impact your life, with (fate permitting) much longer to live?

327   Ella starts living life to the full

Ella found the six months to live exercise very helpful:

'Anxiety about work is always nagging at the top of my mind. However, when I used the six months to live exercise, these once nagging things weren't important at all. The people I loved were, and this practice had me longing for more time to reconnect. I wonder how many other people felt this way after the pandemic?

'Working pays the bills but fretting about work when I'm not there doesn't. I'm going to live my life each day as if I only had six months to live, by genuinely cherishing and nurturing my relationships.'

328   Life is a gift

> 'Life is a gift of the immortal Gods, but living well is
> the gift of philosophy.'
>
> Seneca, *Letters* 90

Imagine you'd won millions in the lottery. How would you feel?

Very excited!

What would you need to do if you won the lottery?

Spend it well!

The good news is that you have already won a much bigger prize than the lottery – being alive.

Do you know the chances of your parents meeting, and then them getting together and conceiving *you*? You need to multiply that by the odds of *their* parents meeting, etc., etc.

It's estimated that the chances of your existing are about *1 in 400 trillion*!

Enjoy this gift!

329   Philosophy is the best use of your time

'By this means alone can you prolong your mortal life,
nay, even turn it into an immortal one.'

Seneca, *On the Shortness of Life* 15

While many leisure pursuits are not such a great use of your time, Stoics believe philosophy is the *best* use of it. This is because it provides the tools to help you live well.

In *On the Shortness of Life*, Seneca waxes lyrical about another benefit of philosophy – that it helps you transcend time:

'The only people who are really at leisure are those who
devote themselves to philosophy: and they alone really live:
for they do not merely enjoy their own lifetime, but they
annex every century to their own: all the years which
have passed before them belong to them.'

On the Shortness of Life 14

Reading these ancient discussions feels a bit like being a guest at a dinner party in 49 CE (toga optional).

330   A morning meditation

This morning, try this meditation. It sums up many of this chapter's key ideas.

1. Wake up with a feeling of gratitude that you have survived to live another day. Then run through how you can best use your time today.

2. Now think on the roles you play in your life and the lives of those you care about (and for). What virtues do you need to fulfil them to the best of your ability?

3. Next, ask what often causes you to waste time and mentally rehearse how you will steer clear of these time-wasters.

4. Finally, remember the odds of your existence. You have won the biggest lottery of all; now make the most of it!

Follow-up

- Redo the diary (**307**: How not to waste your life) to see if your use of time has improved.

- The essential entry in this chapter is **330**: A morning meditation.

- Repeat the exercises in this chapter every year and notice how your thinking develops.

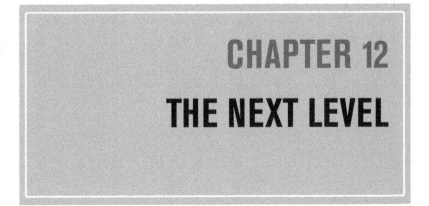

CHAPTER 12

THE NEXT LEVEL

Congratulations! You've discovered 330 ways to be more Stoic! In this closing chapter, you will be learning how to take your Stoicism to the next level.

How Stoic do you want to be? For the advanced beginner – who has read some Epictetus but has yet to read more – Stoicism is all about the dichotomy of control. By now, you know there's much more. So how much of the more advanced Stoic concepts do you want to embrace? Prioritizing character above externals? Stoic physics? Later in this chapter, I'll be introducing the Stoic Elevator framework to help you decide (entries **340–7**).

The final set of entries (**348–60**) is aimed at providing you with the perfect launch pad to continue your Stoic journey after completing this book.

First, I want to introduce Epictetus's three disciplines to help guide and manage your assent, action and desire.

331   The three disciplines

> 'Good judgement, action aimed at the common good,
> and willing acceptance of everything which
> happens – that's all you need.'
>
> Marcus Aurelius, *Meditations* 9.6

Marcus here describes Epictetus's three Stoic disciplines simply in one sentence. We can unwrap them a little:

'Good judgement.' Notice every judgement you make and discard all that are not justified. This is the *discipline of assent* – sometimes also called the discipline of judgement or Stoic mindfulness.

'Action aimed at the common good' – and according to the virtues and the most important roles in your life. This is the *discipline of action*.

'Willing acceptance of everything which happens.' Having appropriate desires and aversions is the *discipline of desire.*

Do you like this quotation as much as I do? Why not memorize it today to help remember the three disciplines? Because, as Marcus says, that's all you need!

332   How well do you know your three disciplines?

Which discipline (assent, action or desire) do these budding Stoics need to work on most?

Jack never says thank you whenever anyone does him a good turn.

Chris has set his heart on getting a pay rise.

Planning a picnic, Judy feels really upset when her friend cancels on her.

Answers:

Action – Jack lacks justice.

Desire – Chris puts too much value on something that is out of his control, not essential to happiness.

Assent – Judy allows the judgement that her friend cancelling was really bad to grow into a grudge.

333   Wise desires: the discipline of desire

The discipline of desire is all about pining for the right things and avoiding the path that leads to dissatisfaction (e.g. drugs, toxic relationships). Ultimately, it's about valuing the quality of your character over externals.

You've learned a lot about how to do this. Here's a reminder of some key entries:

12 – The Stoic Archer – it's fine to aim at 'externals', like the archer aims at the target. Just don't get too upset if you miss – that was outside your control.

19 – A lot of unhappiness is caused by trying to control the uncontrollable.

54 – The dichotomy of value – your character matters more than externals.

103 – Develop life goals that are under your control and consistent with your key roles.

129 – Pleasure is fleeting and can often come at a high cost.

Check/tick the ones you have applied to give yourself a mark out of 5. What do you need to do to progress?

334   Voluntary discomfort

'Set aside a certain number of days, during which you shall be content with the scantiest and cheapest fare, with course and rough dress, saying to yourself the while: "Is this the condition that I feared?"'

Seneca, *Letters*, 18.5

Voluntarily embracing discomfort is a good Stoic technique to help moderate your desires. For a set period (I suggest a week), try one or more of the following:

- eat simple food
- take cold showers
- drink only water
- walk wherever possible.

Before you start, make a prediction about how you will feel and write it down. Keep a note of how your feelings changed over the week.

You might discover that voluntary discomfort isn't what you feared, and that pleasure is overrated.

335   Stoic mindfulness: the discipline of assent

'Attend well to what is at present before you; whether it be a maxim, an action, or the meaning of what someone says.'

Marcus Aurelius, *Meditations* 8.22

The discipline of assent is all about noticing your thoughts, especially your value judgements, and making rational decisions about how to deal with them. You can see why it's also called 'Stoic mindfulness'. These entries explain its essence.

68 – When you have an unhelpful thought, repeat to yourself: 'That's just my initial impression.'

69 – Think of yourself as passport control to guard against snap judgements.

76 – Understand that there is a good and bad a way of handling things – 'Everything has two handles.'

141 – Pause before acting out an unhelpful impulse.

159 – Prioritize the virtues and become less concerned about everything else.

Again, tot up how many of these you have applied to give yourself a mark out of 5.

What do you need to do to progress?

336 Preferences versus demands

Rational emotive behaviour therapy (REBT) – which was created after its founder, Albert Ellis, read Epictetus – makes a valuable distinction between preferences and demands.

It's fine to *prefer* something, but not to *demand* it. So, while it's OK to prefer to want that pay rise, it's not OK to *demand* that it happen. What rule of the universe says you should get everything you want? It's the spoilt child within us that is so demanding. Instead, let the adult within you rule and simply *prefer* things.

337 Behaving like a Stoic: the discipline of action

'First, do nothing inconsiderately, nor without a purpose.
Second, make your acts aim solely at a social end.'

Marcus Aurelius, *Meditations* 12.20

The discipline of action is all about *behaving* like a Stoic. Here are some key entries:

10 – Make a difference by acting with virtue.

106 – Carry out a key roles audit.

153 – Do the right thing right now (even if it involves risk or discomfort).

186 – Expand your concern to other people.

204 – Be a citizen of the world and aim for the common good.

How many of these ideas have you implemented? How can you progress?

338   Which discipline should I work on?

There's a strong case for *all* the disciplines being important:

Desire should have you wanting only the right things.

Assent aids you in making the right judgements.

Action enables you to do the right things.

So perhaps you should work on all the disciplines, prioritizing the one that you scored lowest on when tallying up your marks out of 5 for each discipline.

However, Epictetus argues that desire should be worked on first. We experience negative emotions when we don't get what we want, or when we get what we should avoid. The weight of negative emotion makes it hard to do the right thing (*Discourses* 3.2.2).

If you haven't mastered the discipline of desire, you are asking a lot of the other disciplines. Your life will resemble Whack-A-Mole, constantly challenging unhelpful judgements and using willpower to override unhelpful desires.

Do you agree?

339   How Stoic are you?

For the following statements give yourself a mark from 0 to 4 where 0 = Disagree totally; 1 = Disagree a bit; 2 = Neutral or don't know; 3 = Mainly agree; and 4 = Completely agree.

1. I control the controllables.

2. I let go of those things I can't control.

3. I cultivate the virtues of wisdom, courage, self-control and justice.

4. I think about the virtues when deciding what to do. ☐

5. I am good at dealing with negative and unhelpful thoughts. ☐

6. I am good at managing my emotions. ☐

7. When deciding what to do, I prioritize preserving my character over externals. ☐

8. I extend my concern beyond myself to others and aim for the common good. ☐

9. The cosmos is rational, orderly and benevolent. ☐

10. We are made for co-operation with each other like the rows of upper and lower teeth. ☐

Score yourself out of 40 – the higher your score, the more Stoic you are.

340 The Stoic Elevator

Imagine you are invited to get into a special elevator, one that takes you on a journey through Stoicism. Here's what you'll find on each level:

Level 1 – *The dichotomy of control*

Level 2 – *Cultivating the virtues*

Level 3 – *Managing emotions*

Level 4 – *The dichotomy of value*

Level 5 – *Stoic physics*

The first two statements in 339 are about the dichotomy of control (Level 1). The next two are about cultivating the virtues, and so on. So, by completing 339, you can see how far you've gone up the Stoic Elevator.

How much do you score (out of 8) for each level?

How far up do you want to go?

341 How far up the Stoic Elevator should you go?

Many aspiring Stoics get off the elevator at Level 3. They struggle with Stoic physics and the dichotomy of value.

Does this matter? I know what Epictetus would say …

Our research can shed some empirical light on this question. It suggests that people do benefit a lot from *each* level of the elevator. So just by applying the dichotomy of control, you benefit substantially. But the higher you go, the greater the benefits. People who go all the way to the top will most likely have significantly reduced anxiety and stress and will find long-term happiness easier to achieve.

So why not ride the Stoic Elevator all the way?

342 Keep your integrity

Do you remember the story about the Stoic fighter-pilot, James Bond Stockdale (260)? How the dichotomy of control and reflection on his role helped him avoid being used by the enemy for propaganda?

That's not the whole story, though. Stockdale recalled another passage from Epictetus:

> 'Who is my master? Whoever controls
> what you desire or dislike.'
>
> *Discourses* 2.2

Stockdale understood that he would be lost if he gave any consideration to comfort. Without his focus on integrity, how could he have resisted silver-tongued 'requests' like 'Just record this one speech for us and we will take you out of leg irons'?

Similarly, if you give too much prominence to money or other externals, then you are likely lost down a slippery slope. Watch *Breaking Bad* or *Ozark* if you need convincing …

As Epictetus said, you decide what price you place on your integrity – but for God's sake, don't sell it cheap (*Discourses* 1.2.33)!

343   *Amor fati* for agnostics

> 'There are more things in heaven and Earth, Horatio, /
> Than are dreamt of in your philosophy.'
>
> William Shakespeare, *Hamlet* 1.5.167–8

Human knowledge is too limited to know how the universe works. We can't know if everything is for the best. If everything is for the best, as Stoics argue, then loving your fate, *amor fati*, is appropriate.

If this belief turns out to be false, then *amor fati* will still help you feel less distressed and find more meaning from adversity.

Is this a knockdown argument for *amor fati*, even without embracing Stoic physics?

344   Meditations from a hospital bed

I recently had a spell in the hospital. (I'm fine now, thanks.) I was in awe. The hospital, and the NHS of which it was a part, functioned so well. Every porter, nurse, doctor, receptionist, cook and cleaner played their part.

When I started to feel better, I dipped into Marcus Aurelius's *Meditations*:

> 'Consider the universe as one living being or animal … what a
> connection there is among all things.'
>
> *Meditations* 4.40

I started to imagine the hospital as a living being. (No, I wasn't suffering from delirium.)

If everyone does their job, the organism – the hospital, the NHS – flourishes. Every random act of kindness creates a positive ripple. But if someone pulls a sickie, or communicates thoughtlessly, everyone suffers.

It's helpful to see the interconnectedness of everything and the part we must play.

What parts can *you* play?

345   All the way up the Stoic Elevator

Mary, an enthusiastic horse rider in her twenties, now uses a wheelchair after a riding accident. Imagine versions of Mary that have got off the 'Stoic Elevator' at different levels. How could Stoicism help her in each case?

Here's one possible answer:

Level 1 – The dichotomy of control

Mary will avoid dwelling on 'why me?' and will focus on what is still up to her.

Level 2 – Virtues

Mary will find courage to deal with pain and overcome the challenges of disability.

Level 3 – Managing emotions

Mary will notice and challenge negative thoughts and avoid overgeneralizing or catastrophizing.

Level 4 – The dichotomy of value

Mary will understand that her disability does not affect her capacity to be a good person, and what she has lost are just indifferents.

Mary would clearly benefit from going all the way up the elevator. Out of the five levels, which do you think she'll find most beneficial?

346   Insights from the top!

Think of a current issue and jot down how each level of the Stoic Elevator provides a helpful perspective.

Level 1 – The dichotomy of control

Level 2 – Cultivating the virtues

Level 3 – Managing emotions

Level 4 – The dichotomy of value

_____

_____

Level 5 – Stoic physics

_____

_____

Taking each level into account, where should the elevator take you?

347　Elevator or symphony?

I hope you've found the idea of a Stoic Elevator helpful, but please don't take the 'elevator' metaphor too literally. In truth, the levels don't operate in isolation but interact harmoniously. We saw this in 345, where practising _amor fati_ transformed Mary's acceptance of her disability into something much more positive. Similarly, the dichotomy of value provides extra 'oomph' to Stoic management of emotions, since she is less distressed by what does not damage her character, such as her disability. Marcus Aurelius would say that unless it has ruined your character, it has not ruined your life.

My colleague Chuck Chakrapani has compared Stoicism to a symphony. I like the sound of that. Each element on its own is great, like the individual works of John, Paul, George and Ringo (well, maybe not Ringo _quite_ so much). Put them together and they become the Fab Four, or, in the case of Stoicism, the Fab Five.

The whole is greater than the sum of the parts.

348   Create a Stoic library

It's great to have your own copies of the Stoic classics, but which translations?

I would choose A. A. Long's translation of Epictetus's *Handbook* as *How to be Free: An Ancient Guide to the Stoic Life* (Princeton University Press, 2018) and read it alongside Massimo Pigliucci's revisioning, *A Field Guide to the Happy Life: 53 Brief Lessons for Living* (Basic Books, 2020).

For Epictetus's *Discourses*, I suggest Chuck Chakrapani's *Stoic Inspirations: Epictetus' Fragments, Golden Sayings & Enchiridion* (Stoic Gym, 2018), volume 5 of the *Stoicism in Plain English* series.

My favourite translation of Marcus Aurelius's *Meditations* is by Gregory Hays (Random House, 2004).

Seneca wrote a lot! I would start with the Penguin editions entitled *Letters from a Stoic: Epistulae Morales Ad Lucilium*, translated Robin Campbell, and *Essays and Dialogues*, translated C. Costa.

There are some great books by Modern Stoics to choose from. I'd personally recommend:

Massimo Pigliucci, *How to Be a Stoic* (Basic Books, 2014)

Massimo Pigliucci and Greg Lopez, *Live Like a Stoic: 52 Exercises for Cultivating a Good Life* (Ebury, 2020)

Donald Robertson, *How to Think Like a Roman Emperor: The Stoic Philosophy of Marcus Aurelius* (St. Martin's Press, 2020)

John Sellars, *Lessons in Stoicism: What Ancient Philosophers Teach Us about How to Live* (Penguin, 2020)

There are also a lot of good Stoic websites, including *Modern Stoicism* (https://modernstoicism.com) – home of *Stoic Week* and the *Stoicism*

Today blog. The Aurelius Foundation (https://aureliusfoundation.com) is doing great things to pave the way for the future of Stoicism, spreading awareness and inspiring leadership. The Stoic Fellowship (https://www.stoicfellowship.com/) aims to build, foster and connect Stoic communities around the world. Stoicare (https://www.stoicare.com/) emphasises that Stoicism is a philosophy of care and contains many useful resources.

349   Focus on the virtues

From Chris Gill – Emeritus Professor of Ancient Thought at the University of Exeter and one of the founders of Modern Stoicism

How can I tell whether I am making progress and becoming more Stoic?

Here is one way. Think about whether you are getting better at understanding what it means to live 'according to virtue'; that is, to act in line with virtues like wisdom, courage, moderation and justice. Reflect on whether your improved understanding has affected the way you manage your own life and also the way you treat other people.

350   Create good habits

From John Sellars – author of *Lessons in Stoicism* and one of the founder members (and currently chair) of Modern Stoicism

Epictetus advised that the real goal is trying to break old, bad habits in both how we think and how we act, replacing them with better, new ones. The way to develop a new habit is simply by doing the thing that you want to become habitual. If you want to write, write. If you want to learn how to cook, start cooking. Even the smallest, most amateurish first step is a step in the right direction and, as an old saying goes, every journey starts with one step. Before long, a few first steps will start to develop into something greater.

351   Stoicism at the supermarket

'The palace of reason is reached through the courtyard of habit.'

Richard Peters (1966)

You can practise Stoicism anywhere, even at the supermarket! For example:

- Someone takes your parking space – see it as a Stoic test.
- You are trying to adhere to new dietary restrictions but are craving junk food – a Stoic opportunity to practise (relative) discomfort and self-control.
- There's a long queue at the checkout – a Stoic opportunity to build patience and self-control.

Every difficulty is an opportunity to build a good Stoic habit.

352   Choose your company well

From John Sellars

Epictetus advised students to pay attention to the company they kept and the information they digested. If you are surrounded by examples of bad behaviour or constantly consuming information that distracts you from making progress, then it won't be a surprise if you struggle. So, pay attention to whom and what you spend time with; try to remove negative influences and prioritize good ones.

353   Remember you must die

From Eve Riches – Stoic mentor and co-facilitator of *Stoic Week*

The practical tip I use most often is *memento mori*, in that I say it every time that I can feel myself reacting to a situation and I need to pull back and look at the bigger picture. So, I actually say to myself, 'Remember you must die', as it puts everything in perspective and allows all the other techniques and ideas to be used.

It's why I have that big tattoo of it: it brings me back into the present moment and means I can (usually!) rise above the situation.

354 Start with anger

From Donald Robertson – founder member of Modern Stoicism and the author of several books on Stoicism including *Verissimus: The Stoic Philosophy of Marcus Aurelius*

Start applying Stoicism to your anger. Depressed and anxious people tend to blame themselves, but angry people blame everyone else and often don't think they need to change. The ancient Stoics thought anger was the passion we most urgently need to address. Because it's so neglected, I think of it as the 'royal road to self-improvement' – it's where the biggest gains can usually be made.

355 Be kind to yourself

From Greg Sadler – editor of the *Stoicism Today* blog and a member of the Modern Stoicism team

As you are deliberately trying to incorporate Stoic principles and practices into your ongoing life, at first you are likely to fail a lot. That is entirely normal and happens to most people learning something new. Instead of wasting energy beating yourself up, berating yourself, or feeling bad about those instances of failure, you can remind yourself that you are after all an aspiring Stoic. You are a *prokopton*, someone who is making progress, rather than the legendary sage. And the progress you have made so far isn't nullified by any mistake or lapse, or even backsliding on your part. What you choose to do with that failure after it happens, that's where you have a real opportunity to make more progress.

356   Find your own Stoic path

From Andi Sciacca – Associate Professor of Humanities at the Milwaukee Institute of Art & Design (MIAD) and a member of the Modern Stoicism team

> 'No great thing comes into being suddenly, any more than a bunch of grapes or a fig.'
>
> Epictetus, *Discourses* 1.15.8

I was on the academic decathlon team in high school. Passages from Epictetus were included in our study packs, and I remember feeling deeply called to them. Not even being the age of 17 yet, however, I was naturally focused on other things.

I would meet Epictetus many times after that – along with others like Seneca and Marcus Aurelius. They appeared in my philosophy class, my classical literature class, even my Latin class; I translated the passages but didn't quite internalize the meanings.

In fact, nothing took root until much later, when I found myself frustrated by my own habits. I let anything that went wrong unsettle me and I was miserable. I started to question my belief that more control over my circumstances would help me 'fix' things. It was at that point that I first enrolled in *Stoic Week*. Through a process of daily study and practice, I rekindled that deep calling and found my way back. I can honestly say that my life is much richer and more rewarding as a result.

357   Teach Stoicism, like Epictetus

From Andy Small – a teacher of Stoicism as part of his work in prisons

Do you remember the story of Jay (264)? Here's how Jay got to find out about Stoicism.

My team and I have been teaching Stoicism at HMP Huntercombe for the last five years. Hundreds of prisoners have been on our programmes, with some great successes. Jay was a former county lines drug dealer, organizing young people to sell drugs in the suburbs of London and surrounding towns. He completed the Stoic course and became a practising Stoic. Upon release, he went on to work in full-time crime prevention at Charlton Athletic Football Club.

Since then, Jay has spoken to over a thousand young people in his community in London, teaching them some Stoic principles to help them avoid the drug-selling lifestyle that became his downfall. Jay continues to be a practising Stoic, a practising Muslim and a better father than he has ever been.

358   Journal like Marcus, write like Seneca

From Meredith Alexander Kunz – writer and speaker on Stoicism and author of *The Stoic Mom* blog

Marcus Aurelius's personal journal became the *Meditations*. Seneca wrote essays and letters of advice to his friends.

Two of the most important Stoic practices in my life are reading and writing. I read ancient texts and modern interpretations, and I write about applying Stoic ideas in my blog *The Stoic Mom*.

When I heard about the Odes to Marcus Aurelius competition (organized by Modern Stoicism in honour of Marcus's 1900th birthday), I knew I wanted to create a special piece of writing for this occasion. I envisioned writing a poem inspired by the ancient book that I return to again and again – Marcus Aurelius's *Meditations*. Sitting in my backyard, a leafy refuge during the global pandemic, words came flowing out. I worked to capture the essence of the Stoic emperor's reflections in just 250 words. My poem 'Make Yourself Good' was the result. I continue to turn back to this short piece when I need a reminder of what really matters. It begins like this:

> 'Do not act as if you had ten thousand years to live.'
> Marcus Aurelius, *Meditations* 4.17

> Remember that this moment
> Is all you have:
> Each flying second
> Your personal eternity
> To make with it
> What you can
> On this earth.

359   Stoicism in the arts

I love looking out for Stoicism in films, music and poetry.

The films *Life Is Beautiful*, *Casablanca* and *The Shawshank Redemption* all contain Stoic themes. But my favourite film to see through the lens of Stoicism is *Groundhog Day*. Its hero, Phil Connors, is the perfect example of *oikeiôsis*, as reliving the same day repeatedly helps him to understand what he can and cannot control, enabling him to become a better, happier human being in the end. (See https://modernstoicism. com/the-stoicism-of-groundhog-dayby-tim-lebon/)

Music too can provide memorable Stoic insights. Next time you hear 'Raindrops Keep Fallin' on My Head', 'Let It Be' or 'Imagine', think of their potential Stoic meaning.

Quick Stoic poetry quiz!

Which Stoic-influenced poems include the lines:

a. 'I am the master of my fate / I am the captain of my soul.'

b. 'If you can keep your head, when all about you / Are losing theirs and blaming it on you.'

Answers:

a. 'Invictus' by Rupert Hanley

b. 'If' by Rudyard Kipling – my favourite!

---

360   If you can be a Stoic (with apologies to Kipling)

If you can accept everything not up to you,
Feel gratitude, no matter what your fate,
If you can act well, and according to nature,
Love everybody, even those who hate,
If you can be mindful of all your impressions,
Asking each – are you what you claim to be?
Then you will be a happy Stoic, my good friend.
Wise desires, wise actions, wise judgements – and free.

Follow-up

- Have another go at the self-assessments in this chapter (**333**, **335**, **337** and **339**) and compare your scores with what they were previously.

- The essential entry in this chapter is **346**: Insights from the top!

- Decide which tips you most want to take forward. Plan how to make it happen.

EPILOGUE:

THE 'BIG FIVE' TAKEAWAYS

361 Focus on what you can control and let go of everything else

Some things are under your control and others are not. You can't change this fact, but you can change how you deal with it. If you try to change what you cannot control, you will become frustrated and ineffective. When you channel all your energy into what you can control – the way you think about things and what you do – then you will become more effective and, our research suggests, much more full of zest.

362 Concentrate on your character, which is your royal road to happiness

Many seek happiness in the wrong places. Sure, a new car, lover or promotion might bring a temporary thrill – but how long will that last? Only things chosen wisely have a chance of providing lasting happiness. What's more, you need the right skills – the character qualities called the virtues – to maintain these things. You need courage to keep going when the going gets tough, self-control to avoid short-termism, and justice to get on well with other people. Surprisingly, happiness is less likely achieved by following the paths most advertised in modern times than by developing the ageless virtues of wisdom, courage, self-control and justice.

363 It's not events that affect you, it's your interpretations of events

Many assume that if things don't go to plan, then they are bound to get upset. But if this were true, how could it be true that the same event – such as being turned down for a job – impacts people in such different ways? Someone might reflect that it's normal to get rejected sometimes, others assume that this means that they have no prospects. Same event, different way of thinking about it, different emotions. To change how you feel, change how you think.

364 See difficulties as Stoic challenges and opportunities

Next time life throws you a curve ball, see it as an opportunity to build your resilience. For example, next time you are stuck in traffic, choose to see this as a Stoic challenge. How could you hope to improve your ability to handle difficulties if you don't get a chance to practise?

365 Stoicism is about doing things, not just accepting things – practise a little Stoicism every day to work towards becoming the best version of you

How do you develop any skill? *Practise.*

How often should you practise? *Regularly.*

How can you best build on what you've learned in this book? Here's one way that I'm confident would reap benefits.

In the morning, spend ten minutes reading – or rereading – an entry that feels relevant to your current concerns. Look for opportunities to put what you've learned into practice throughout the day. Towards the end of the day, spend a few moments reflecting on how the day has gone and what you can learn from it.

But that's just one way. There are many, many – perhaps as many as 365 – ways to become more Stoic.

REFERENCES

The following translations of classic Stoic works were chosen because of rights restrictions. See entry 348: Create a Stoic library for recommended modern translations.

Classical Stoic texts

Note: Translations have sometimes been modernized or otherwise amended for clarity.

Epictetus (1758). *All the works of Epictetus.* Translated E. Carter. S. Richardson.

Epictetus (1890). *The works of Epictetus, consisting of his Discourses in four books.* Translated T. W. Higginson. Little, Brown, & Co.

Epictetus (1916). *The Discourses and Manual, together with fragments of his writings.* 3 vols. Translated P. E. Matheson. Clarendon Press.

Epictetus (1955). *The Philosophy of Epictetus.* Translated J. Bonforte, based on the translation of T. W. Higginson. Philosophical Library.

Marcus Aurelius (1742). *The Meditations of the Emperor Marcus Aurelius Antoninus.* Edited and translated F. Hutcheson and J. Moor. Liberty Fund.

Marcus Aurelius (1862). *The thoughts of M. Aurelius.* 2nd ed. Edited and translated G. Long. George Bell & Sons.

Marcus Aurelius (1968). *Meditations.* Edited and translated A. S. L. Farquharson. Oxford University Press.

Seneca (1920). *Of a happy life.* In *Minor dialogues together with the dialogue 'On Clemency'.* Translated A. Stewart. Bohn's Classical Library Edition. George Bell & Sons.

Other references

Becker, L. C. A. (2017). *A New Stoicism*. Revised edition. Princeton University Press.

Biswas-Diener, R. (2012). *The Courage Quotient*. Jossey-Bass.

Chakrapani, C. & LeBon, T. (2011). *Stoicism: Cobwebs and Gems*. The Stoic Gym.

Clark, D. M. & Wells, A. (1995). A cognitive model of social phobia. In R. Heimberg, M. Liebowitz, D. A. Hope & F. R. Schneier (Eds.), *Social Phobia: Diagnosis, Assessment, and Treatment*. New York: Guilford Press.

Covey, S. (1992). *The 7 Habits of Highly Effective People*. Simon & Schuster.

Csikszentmihalyi, M. (1990). *Flow: The Psychology of Optimal Experience*. Rider.

Duffy, K. (2020). *Backbone: An Inspirational Manual for Coping with Chronic Pain*. Arcade Publishing.

Emmons, R. (2003). Personal goals, life meaning, and virtue: Wellsprings of a positive life. In C. L. M. Keyes & J. Haidt (Eds.), *Flourishing: Positive Psychology and the Life Well Lived* (pp. 105–128). American Psychological Association. https://doi.org/10.1037/10594-005. Available at: http://www.psychology.hku.hk/ftbcstudies/refbase/docs/emmons/2003/53_Emmons2003.pdf

Emmons, R. A. & Shelton, C. S. (2002). Gratitude and the science of positive psychology. In C. R. Snyder and S. J. Lopez (Eds.), *Handbook of Positive Psychology* (pp. 459–471). Oxford University Press.

Fowler, S. (2020). *Whistleblower: My Journey to Silicon Valley and Fight for Justice*. Penguin.

Frankl, V. (1946). *Man's Search for Meaning*. Hodder.

Gill, C. & LeBon, C. (2017). A Stoic values clarification dialogue and workshop. Modern Stoicism. https://modernstoicism.com/a-stoic-values-clarification-dialogue-and-workshop-by-christopher-gill-and-tim-lebon/

Holiday, R. (2014). *The Obstacle is the Way*. Profile Books.

Johnson, B. (2013). *The Role Ethics of Epictetus*. Lexington Books.

Kahneman, D. (2011). *Thinking Fast and Slow*. Farrar, Straus and Giroux.

LeBon, T. (2014). *Achieve Your Potential with Positive Psychology*. Hodder.

Mischel, W. (2015). *The Marshmallow Test*. Corgi.

Park, N., Peterson, C. & Seligman, M. E. P. (2004). Strengths of character and well-being. *Journal of Social and Clinical Psychology*, 23(5):603–619. https://doi.org/10.1521/jscp.23.5.603.50748

Pausch, R. (2008). *The Last Lecture*. Hyperion.

Peters, R. S. (1966). *Ethics and Education*. Routledge.

Pigliucci, M. (2020). *The Stoic Guide to a Happy Life*. Rider.

Seligman, M. (2002). *Authentic Happiness*. Nicholas Brealey.

Steger, M. F., Kashdan, T. B. & Oishi, S. (2008). Being good by doing good: Daily eudaimonic activity and well-being. *Journal of Research in Personality*, 42(1):22–42. https://doi.org/10.1016/j.jrp.2007.03.004

Stockdale J. B. (1993) *Courage Under Fire*. Hoover.

Sullivan. M. and Blaschko, P. (2022) *The Good Life Method*. Penguin.

Wegner, D. (1989.) *White Bears and Other Unwanted Thoughts*. Guilford Press.

Worthington, E. (2020) The science of forgiveness. https://www.templeton.org/wp-content/uploads/2020/06/Forgiveness_final.pdf

Yalom, I. (1989). *Love's Executioner*. Penguin.

ACKNOWLEDGEMENTS

Thank you to the following persons for their contributions to this book:

Alison McCone, 2022

Andi Sciacca, 2022

Andy Small, 2021

Brittany Polat, 2022

Carmelo Di Maria, 2022

Christopher Gill, 2021

Chuck Chakrapani, 2022

David Arnaud, 2022

Eric Weiner, 2022

Eve Riches, 2022

Gregory Lopez, 2022

Gregory B. Sadler, 2022

Jay Adam, 2022

John Harlow, 2022

John Sellars, 2022

Justin Stead, 2022

Kai Whiting, 2022

Kasey Pierce, 2022

Keith Seddon, 2022

Lori Huica, 2022

Megan Brown, 2022

Meredith Alexander Kunz, 2022

Paul Blaschko, 2022

Paul Wilson, 2022

Peter Cooper, 2022

Phil Yanov, 2022

Piotr Stankiewicz, 2022

Ranjini George, 2022

Ronald W. Pies, 2022

Scott Corey, 2022

Scott Perry, 2022

Shamil Chandaria, 2022

Sylvia Pierce, 2022

Trevor Munro-Clark, 2022

Walter J. Matweychuk, PhD, 2022

IT'S TIME TO SEIZE THE DAY.
ALL 365 OF THEM.

365 – your day-by-day guide to living better and working smarter

365 Ways to be More Stoic 978-1-52939-044-5

365 Ways to Develop Mental Toughness 978-1-52939-764-2

365 Ways to Save the Planet 978-1-52939-741-3

365 Ways to Live Mindfully 978-1-52939-039-1

365 Ways to Have a Good Day 978-1-52938-224-2

365 WAYS TO HAVE A GOOD DAY

By Ian Sanders

365 WAYS TO HAVE A GOOD DAY is a full year's worth of daily inspiration, tools, habits, actions, and rituals that will help you live your best life. You'll discover surprising insights from psychologists, business leaders, entrepreneurs and designers. You'll explore the benefits of Feierabends and Laughies, have your eyes opened by a dance psychologist, and find out why one senior executive's tattooed fingers help him make the right career choices.

"An inspiring, heart-warming, go-getting book ... an antidote to apathy."

Helen Tupper, co-author of *The Squiggly Career*

Hardback 978-1-52938-224-2

272pp 198×129mm

365 WAYS TO LIVE MINDFULLY

By Pascale Engelmajer

365 WAYS TO LIVE MINDFULLY contains a full year's worth of daily inspiration, stories, practices, exercises and meditations that will help you live more mindfully. You'll learn ways to focus your attention on your present experience, to be fully in the moment, and to create a life that's consistent with your values and aspirations. You'll develop habit-forming strategies, pick up helpful concepts, and discover tips for lasting change.

Hardback 978-1-52939-039-1

240pp 198×129mm

Would you like your people to read this book?

If you would like to discuss how you could bring these ideas to your team, we would love to hear from you. Our titles are available at competitive discounts when purchased in bulk across both physical and digital formats. We can offer bespoke editions featuring corporate logos, customized covers, or letters from company directors in the front matter can also be created in line with your special requirements.

We work closely with leading experts and organizations to bring forward-thinking ideas to a global audience. Our books are designed to help you be more successful in work and life.

For further information, or to request a catalogue, please contact:
business@johnmurrays.co.uk
sales-US@nicholasbrealey.com (North America only)

John Murray Learning is an imprint of
John Murray Press.